More TALES FOR TRAINERS

More TALES FOR TRAINERS

Using stories and metaphors to influence and encourage learning

MARGARET PARKIN

KoganPage

LONDON PHILADELPHIA NEW DELHI

Publisher's note

Every possible effort has been made to ensure that the information contained in this book is accurate at the time of going to press, and the publishers and author cannot accept responsibility for any errors or omissions, however caused. No responsibility for loss or damage occasioned to any person acting, or refraining from action, as a result of the material in this publication can be accepted by the editor, the publishers or the author.

First published in Great Britain and the United States in 2010 by Kogan Page Limited

120 Pentonville Road	525 South 4th Street, #241	4737/23 Ansari Road
London N1 9JN	Philadelphia PA 19147	Daryaganj
United Kingdom	USA	New Delhi 110002
www.koganpage.com		India

© Margaret Parkin, 2010

The right of Margaret Parkin to be identified as the author of this work has been asserted by her in accordance with the Copyright, Designs and Patents Act 1988.

ISBN   978 0 7494 6085 3
E-ISBN   978 0 7494 6086 0

British Library Cataloguing-in-Publication Data

A CIP record for this book is available from the British Library.

Library of Congress Cataloging-in-Publication Data

Parkin, Margaret.
    More tales for trainers : using stories and metaphors to influence and encourage learning / Margaret Parkin. -- 1st ed.
        p. cm.
    Includes bibliographical references and index.
    ISBN 978-0-7494-6085-3 -- ISBN 978-0-7494-6086-0 1. Employees--Training of. 2. Employee training personnel--Training of. 3. Storytelling--Study and teaching--Activity programs. I. Title.
    HF5549.5.T7P2817 2010
    658.3'124--dc22
                                            2010017880

Typeset by Saxon Graphics Ltd, Derby
Printed and bound in India by Replika Press Pvt Ltd

Contents

induction programme 69; Using stories before a training session 70; Unfinished stories and nested stories 71; Using stories for group discussion 71; Using stories for illustrative purposes 72; Using stories for evaluation 73; Ending the day with a story 74; Using different types of story for different effects 74; How to find stories 76; Telling the tale – incorporating the storyteller's skills 78; Bring the story alive through use of voice 82; Non-verbal communication 83; Don't think you have to be perfect 84; To sum up... 85

Introduction

It was a seemingly impossible task – to be given the last slot of the day with a large and boisterous group of mature MBA students, who had completed their weekend of practical assignments, completed their dissertations, and now just wanted to go home. An impossible task – to entertain, inspire, enlighten … actually just keeping 70 people quiet in one room was quite a feat. No sooner had I managed to calm one side of the room than the other would burst forth into more excited chatter – indeed, it started to feel a little like trying to keep a number of spinning plates in place. The participants feigned polite interest in the topic that I had been allocated – powerful communication skills – but it was only towards the end of the hour-long session (and possibly out of desperation), that I decided to tell them a story … and then something rather strange happened.

One by one, the animated conversations on each of the dozen or so tables simply seemed to peter out and die, and I found, to my surprise, that my storytelling was greeted by complete and rapt attention. The change in atmosphere was so pronounced that, at the end of the session, rather than leaping out of their chairs like rockets as I thought they would have done, no one moved. I actually had to tell them that they could go home. From that day, I began to realize that there was something special about storytelling. I discovered that stories do something that other forms of communication fail to do: they completely engage an audience – and they can *actually change behaviour*.

But what does this story have to do with my organization, I hear you say? What does it tell me about furthering my organization's aims? If there has been any good outcome at all from the recent world recession, it has been to teach people in organizations that we cannot go on with a 'business as usual' approach, doing the same things and hoping that business will pick up. Sadly, we are now operating in a climate of mistrust – we have lost our faith in politicians, bankers and other figures of authority. We no longer believe in the spam emails (if we ever did) telling us we've won a million dollars; we are weary with information overload.

Today's organizations have to start to rebuild trust, both internally and externally, and find different, creative and authentic ways of communicating and engaging with staff, customers and other stakeholders.

Business narrative or storytelling provides one of those means of engagement; uniquely, stories work through speaking to both parts of the human mind – reason and emotion – which is what makes them such a powerful communication and influencing method. Increasingly, various organizations throughout the world are realizing this potential – not just in the area of learning and development but also in research, PR and marketing, branding and culture change. Firms such as Eli Lilly, Cadbury, Nike, Johnson & Johnson, NASA, Twinings, Lego and Hewlett-Packard are all benefiting from the added ROI that storytelling can bring – both inside and outside the organization. One previously rather dull comparison website in the UK created a bizarre but loveable character called Aleksandr Orlov, an aristocratic Russian meerkat, to head up their advertising campaign – and, according to an article in *Marketing Magazine* (www.marketingmagazine.co.uk), have seen their sales rocket by 70 per cent. Who said storytelling was frivolous?

Trainers, coaches, HR and OD consultants are playing a vital role in this regeneration process; many are now more involved, as business partners, in the core of their organization's business, becoming instrumental in communicating vision, values and purpose – both of the organization as a whole and also the HR and training functions within it. Trainers particularly are realizing that in their role, the emphasis is now more than ever on meeting the needs of the learner, and on finding more effective, engaging and memorable methods of learning to meet those needs. But more of this in Chapter 1...

So how specifically can using stories and storytelling benefit the trainer, the learner and the organization? In terms of internal communication and learning, stories can:

- communicate the vision and purpose of the organization – the 'core story';
- make values more meaningful and attainable;
- help to define organizational culture;

- be used as a research tool, to lend an insight into the 'health' of an organization;
- encourage the change process by bypassing conscious resistance;
- make the learning process more effective, engaging and memorable;
- encourage reflective, imaginative and productive thinking;
- provide material for knowledge sharing and learning workshops;
- encourage others to get out of habitual thinking patterns by providing a 're-frame';
- develop trust and engagement by providing social proof through posting employee stories on the company intranet.

In terms of external communication with customers, suppliers and other stakeholders, stories can also be used effectively:

- to bring statistics and data to life when used as part of a sales presentation;
- to make presentations more memorable;
- as part of advertising and marketing campaigns;
- to enhance the organization's image;
- to ensure that the organization stands out from the rest;
- as part of an engaging recruitment strategy;
- to develop trust by providing social proof through the use of success stories from existing customers.

The aim of this book is to offer trainers, coaches and OD consultants some further insights and practical methods on how these benefits can be achieved. In Part 1:

Chapter 1 Stories and learning

Describes how stories help us to learn; defines whole-brain and informal learning; how storytelling can help the learning process through patterning and use of imagery; the role of metaphor in learning and change; choosing the right metaphor; conscious and unconscious learning.

Chapter 2 How stories influence

Looks at the psychological basis of stories; why we tell stories at all; how stories influenced us as children and still do today; the effects stories have on people's minds; the advantages of story over facts and figures alone; stories and emotion; how to influence, motivate and mobilize using stories.

Chapter 3 Sharing the story

Positions stories and metaphors within the organizational context; how to categorize positive and negative stories; the need for consistency between story and action; how stories can define culture; using stories to bring values to life; managing the grapevine; story as a means of knowledge sharing.

Chapter 4 Telling the tale

Provides practical help on when and where (and where not) to use stories; practical uses for inclusion of stories, eg in induction training, to stimulate group discussion; as part of the evaluation process; different stories produce different effects; where to find good stories; how to practise the storyteller's skills eg humour, repetition, exaggeration; how to bring stories to life through use of voice and non-verbal communication.

In Part 2, the collection of 50 tales is designed to encourage reflective thinking and to illustrate the various learning concepts that you, as a trainer, will no doubt find yourself required to address in your management, leadership or personal development training. These concepts might include such areas as: improving relationships between leaders and teams; offering creative solutions to problems; dealing constructively with change; influencing skills; emotional intelligence and managing conflict.

The 50 stories are all carefully selected; although seemingly diverse in their origins, what all of them have in common is that their end purpose is to help you and/or your learners see a situation from a different point of view, which in turn offers an opportunity for learning and the means to react positively and creatively to that situation. Stories such as these promote creative thought and discussion; they are designed to stimulate whole-brain learning, and to enable that learning to be absorbed, remembered and later applied in the workplace. They are mostly quite short, taking five minutes or so in the telling. Some of them draw from the ancient and timeless wisdom of Buddha, the Greek myths or traditional fairy tales, whereas others, no less important, have been gleaned from modern business people.

I have done my best to herd these 50 stories into some sorts of groups, although if you've ever tried herding stories together, you will know that they're not the easiest of things to pin down! Some of them, very tediously to my mind, have kept swapping places from one group to another, and some have quite coquettishly insisted on being placed together. So the three categories below are intended merely as a rough guide. As with all stories, I'm sure you will adapt them and bend them to fit your particular needs.

1. **Enlightening tales.** These are a collection of ancient and modern tales: myths, fables, fairy tales and contemporary stories which, when placed in a business context, help to illuminate organization-related issues. Enlightening tales are intended to help understanding, to increase our knowledge or wisdom and to dispel ignorance. They can shine a light on a difficult or complex topic. These are the tales, which, if you've told them well, will be greeted with an 'Aaaahaaa' sort of sound from your audience – a sure indication that learning has taken place (although of course you don't always know what they've learnt ... which can make evaluation difficult!).

2. **Cautionary tales.** Ever since the days of the ancient fables of Aesop, the cautionary tale was intended to educate and particularly to warn against certain threats that a young person might encounter. The original cautionary tales contained three essential elements: first the introduction of the act, situation or object that is said to be dangerous, then the story in which someone boldly disregards the warnings, and finally the climax of the piece – often with the perpetrator coming to a sticky end. The cautionary tale, by its very nature, often had a less than happy ending – indeed its role was to shock the listener out of complacency. This collection, which includes ancient tales such as 'The goose that laid the golden eggs', 'The fox and the grapes', as well as modern warnings from business people including Dr Peter Honey, can serve as a useful focus for group discussion, or as a vehicle for knowledge sharing.

3. **Happy endings.** In these recent, somewhat sombre, days of recession, stories can relax, surprise or entertain us, make us feel that life is worth living, and just make us laugh. These stories are not meant to be particularly deep or meaningful, so there are no 'Reflection' and 'Talking points' sections after them. However, they can still be used productively during a workshop, as fill-ins, to bridge to your next topic, after lunch (the notorious graveyard

spot) or at the end of a training session, to energize or to leave participants on a high. And of course, there's still nothing to say you can't use them for discussion purposes if you so wish. As the group title suggests, this collection of tales might have a twist or an unexpected, but hopefully happy, ending.

The format for the stories

There are two activity sections that follow the first two categories of stories – 'Reflection' and 'Talking points', which are designed to help you put the story into a business or organizational context and maximize its use as a reflective learning tool. The sections draw from some of the reflective-thinking models developed by Borton (1970), Gibbs (1988), Kolb (1985) and others, the purpose here being to consider:

'What?' (What is the message of the story?)

'So what?' (Does it mean anything to me? Can I relate to this?)

'Now what?' (What can I do with this additional knowledge or understanding?)

Reflection

Although the suggested moral or meaning of the story is included here, be aware that stories can mean different things to different people. Avoid forcing learners into just accepting your interpretation of the moral or meaning of the story; they may have picked up an idea entirely different from yours, which could still be a valid opinion, and could add to the richness of the discussion.

Also included in this section are suggested areas in which the tale might be used, such as managing change, emotional intelligence, perceptions, dealing with conflict, leadership. A full list of topics covered is given below, but of course the final decision as to how the story could best be used is up to you. This list is by no means exhaustive, and you may feel that some of the messages in the stories overlap a number of categories. It is better to take a pragmatic approach, experiment with various stories in different situations and make a note of the response you get. The stories can be used for:

Branding/marketing

Communication

Creativity

Customer care

Dealing with change

Dealing with conflict

Emotional intelligence (understanding self and others)

Empowerment/engagement

Equality and diversity

Ethics

Induction into a new area or job

Influence

Integrity/humility

Knowledge sharing

Leadership

Learning and development

Motivation and reward

Perceptions

Performance management

Positive thinking

Presentation skills

Problem solving

Project management

Realistic goal setting

Self-belief

Strategic planning

Talent management

Teamwork

Talking points

This section helps you to generate productive discussion around the story. There are some suggested 'trigger' questions to get the dialogue going and to give it a semi-structured framework. If working with a group, you might decide to give these questions out to the participants, or alternatively, you might just read out one or two – or add your own. If using the stories in a coaching session, you may want to weave in some questions as part of your natural dialogue. It depends on the context within which you are using the story, what outcome you hope to achieve, the experience of the person or group and how much time you have allocated for the session.

You should always choose your trigger questions wisely: there is a huge difference between asking 'Can you relate this story to your own organization?' and 'How does this story relate to your organization?' The former is the more reflective and open of the two, while the latter forces a connection where there may not be one. I tend to find that the fewer but more open-ended and reflective questions you use with the stories, the better and more creative the response. The more your questions start to look like a list or a comprehension exercise, the more the linear, left brain has the chance to kick in, and you find participants involved in a 'tick box' exercise, with a desire to provide the 'right' answer, rather than allowing themselves time to reflect and ponder.

So, before these stories start to climb off the page, or decide to rearrange themselves just one more time, perhaps we should begin...

Part 1

Once upon a time ...

Stories and learning

'I can't tell you just now what the moral of that is, but I shall remember it in a bit.'

'Perhaps it hasn't one,' Alice ventured to remark.

'Tut, tut, child!' said the Duchess. 'Everything's got a moral, if only you can find it.'

Lewis Carroll, Alice's Adventures in Wonderland *(1865)*

How the role of the trainer has changed

I blush when I think back to the beginning of my career as a trainer some 25 years ago. In those days, your main concern was whether there was a light bulb in the overhead projector (for those who haven't heard of them, these were the things we used before PowerPoint) and hoping that the flip-chart pens wouldn't dry up. Words like 'Training officer', 'instruction', 'lecture', and 'student' were commonplace.

But world changes in the 1990s in globalization, technology and competition brought about the need for organizations to adapt and learn more quickly, and phrases like 'the learning organization' started to creep in, described, among others, by Peter Senge as:

> An organization where people continually expand their capacity to create the results they truly desire, where new and expansive patterns of thinking are nurtured, where collective aspiration is set free, and where people are continually learning how to learn together.

Senge, 1990

Of course, if we're honest, few of us at the time really knew what it meant or what its implications might be; a not-quite-so-eloquent, but probably honest reaction was evidenced by a managing director I was working with at the time, who instructed me: 'We're a learning organization – now get these blighters to learn!' More recently, the Chartered Institute of Personnel and Development (CIPD) Learning and Development survey of 2009 found that 50 per cent of companies canvassed were working towards the integration of a learning and development culture in their organization.

So if the focus in organizations has changed to one of continuous and shared learning, as highlighted by Senge, this means, by implication, that the role of the trainer must also have changed. Now, in the 21st century, the emphasis has shifted away from the trainer and towards the learner, and a whole new vocabulary has evolved. In fact, in some cases the very title 'trainer' has disappeared and metamorphosed into the rather more grandiose-sounding 'Learning and development consultant' – a name that was apparently endlessly debated by the CIPD during its review of professional standards in 1999/2000. Similar deliberations in the United States resulted in other catchy labels including 'Workplace learning and performance professional'. But while other people debate the title, trainers in today's organizations need to get on with doing the job, while at the same time being aware of (and accepting) the changes in demand for their services. Martyn Sloman of the CIPD says:

> Today organizations understand that ongoing learning is an essential element of the modern workplace and it therefore makes sense that trainers adapt themselves and recognize that learning and development will occur with or without them, at any time and in any place... The role of the trainer therefore becomes one of support, direction and acceleration.

So trainers today are just as likely to be coaches, mentors, IT specialists, organizational development consultants as they are teachers or instructors – but above all, as Sloman says, they are managers and supporters of learning, whatever shape that may take.

Informal learning

In today's organizations, although learning still takes place formally in a classroom environment, or with a coach or mentor or at a PC, it also happens informally – 'intentional and incidental' learning (Nadler and Nadler, 1990). In other words, what is taught is not necessarily the same as what learners learn, and is certainly not the whole picture. Some learners claim to glean as much from additional sources – the internet, social and business networking sites such as Facebook and LinkedIn, and sharing their own and others' experiences – as they do from a trainer or formal training programme. Bearing witness to this is the number of evaluation forms I have read over the years that stated 'the best part was meeting all the other delegates', making me realize the truth of this distinction. Although from the trainer's perspective it might be seen as somewhat depressing, this is the reality (and not quite as depressing as the soulful comment I once read: 'I did not like the egg in the sandwiches at lunchtime').

Introducing stories

Learning through sharing stories with others can be a great resource for the trainer, learner and organization; they provide not just an important and cost-effective tool for learning but also for developing relationships with others in one's social group. Anthropologists maintain that as our ancestors evolved to live in groups, they had to make sense of increasingly complex social relationships. And the same is true today as organizations' reporting structures become ever more complex and global; living or working in a community requires an ongoing knowledge of the dynamics within the group, who the 'movers and shakers' are within the group and how to influence and interact with them. An article on 'The secrets of storytelling' by Jeremy Hsu in the *Scientific American Journal* in 2008 said:

> Stories help us to keep tabs on what is happening in our communities. The safe, imaginary world of a story may be a kind of training ground, where we can practice interacting with others and learn the customs and rules of society.

And yet, not all organizational cultures support the sharing of stories or recognize it as a valid means of learning; not all individuals think to pass their knowledge on to colleagues. Stan Garfield, writing in the *Knowledge Management Review* in 2006, identified a number of barriers to passing on of knowledge between team members, among them:

1. not knowing why they should do it;
2. not knowing how to do it, not having been trained;

3. there is no positive consequence or reward for doing it (or worse – that not doing it, ie keeping knowledge to oneself, is seen as having greater currency).

So as trainers or coaches we need to encourage, nurture and manage this activity in the right way, albeit subtly. My experience over the years has shown that probably one of the worst demands you can make, if wanting to encourage participants to share stories is: 'So ... tell me a story about...' Maybe there is something about the word 'story' that makes people freeze; maybe it's about being put on the spot; or maybe it's the misperception that you have to suddenly turn into 'Super Raconteur' and embark on an hour-long monologue that has listeners rolling in the aisles with laughter or gasping with admiration. If you're encouraging people to relay their experiences and share their knowledge in the form of a story, it is an activity best done subtly and almost imperceptibly – as the activities below show.

Learning activity – best and worst

Encourage knowledge sharing through pairs or groups discussing their best and worst experiences of a particular event, say, a performance review, or handling a difficult client, or selling a new product.

Best: what was it about this experience that you remember in a positive light? What did you see, hear and feel?

Worst: what was it about this experience that you remember in a negative way? What did you see, hear, feel? What outcome did you want instead?

Giving participants the freedom and space to talk about their perceptions of 'worst' as well as the 'best' memories lends the process (and you) more credibility. It shows that you are acknowledging the fact that it's normal to have 'off' days and less-than-perfect experiences and are allowing them to vent their true feeling and frustrations. And yet, by managing the activity, the 'worst' stories aren't allowed to descend down the slippery slope into the 'Ain't it awful' valley of despair. The activity is nominally contained and controlled, so that while acknowledging the negatives, we can still turn them into a positive learning opportunity by asking the question 'What did you want instead?' thereby drawing a comparison and focusing on desired outcomes.

I recall using this exercise while working with a group of hotel staff who were considering how their levels of customer service might be improved. One young receptionist started to tell a 'worst' tale of The Impossible Guest, a woman who kept ringing, usually in the middle of the night, to make outlandish requests and lodge complaints about miniscule problems. The conventional approach is for the trainer to say, 'And how should we deal with this type of situation?' applying the rules of good customer care in an almost sanitized fashion. Instead, sensing a raw emotion bubbling away behind the receptionist's voice, I asked, almost in a whisper, 'What would you have liked to have said to her?' She replied, stoically quoting from the procedures manual, 'Well, I should have taken a deep breath...' 'No, no,' I said, whispering even more conspiratorially, 'What would you *really* have liked to say?' This time her face changed, almost into a grimace, and a torrent of abuse poured forth. 'I wanted to tell her to get a ******* life, get off my ******* back, pack her ******* bags, go away and *leave me alone!*' She stopped, breathless and somewhat amazed at the sympathetic laughter and applause that surrounded her. It felt like something had been expunged rather than contained through this honest outburst, which then gave us the freedom to go on and explore the rather more appropriate behaviours that she might have adopted. Annette Simmons, in her book *The Story Factor* (2006), says:

> Deep disillusionment needs to be acknowledged before it can shrink to a manageable size. It is disrespectful to tell someone who is disillusioned to buck up and focus on the positive. Prove that you see what they see, and are still hopeful.

An activity that I call 'Talking points' can offer an informal alternative to the dreaded 'Let's all introduce ourselves' part of a training day or as an opener for a team briefing. The activity consists of a simple series of cards, some of them humorous, and some even contentious in tone, that are intended to stimulate dialogue and encourage knowledge sharing. (Of course, the topics on the cards can be designed to fit your own organization and/or the focus of your training session or meeting.) Depending on the size of the group, you can either carry this out around small tables or with the group as a whole. This activity gives participants a light-hearted and semi-structured focus to the problem of group introductions or the starting point for a meeting, and also lays to rest the notion of 'I can't tell stories.' Colleagues often surprise themselves during this exercise with the amount of information they learn and the information they didn't know about each other.

Learning activity: Talking points

Encourage stories and knowledge sharing with these Talking point cards – some are purely work-related topics, some more personal, some humorous or contentious. Here are some examples that I used with staff at a Heritage Centre in the north of England:

- What has been the highlight of your last 12 months?
- Describe the time you worked the hardest.
- If you could be invisible for the day, what would be the first thing you would do?
- Who has been the funniest visitor you have had? Why?
- Have you ever been tempted to misdirect a visitor, tell them a lie or exaggerate?

Whole-brain learning

As well as capitalizing on the information that can be gleaned through informal learning, trainers also need to be aware that, if their organization is moving ever more quickly and innovatively to keep ahead of the competition, they too must look for creative learning methods that will accommodate and support that process. This means that the ways in which trainers understand and encourage the learning process may also change. Daniel Pink, in his book *A Whole New Mind* (2008), talks of the move away from an economy built on the 'logical, linear, computer-like capabilities of the Information Age' towards an economy that is built on 'the inventive, empathetic, big-picture capabilities of the Conceptual Age' – which in turn requires a different approach to how we regard the brain's function as a learning tool.

We know, from the work carried out by the likes of Roger Sperry and Ned Hermann from the 1960s onwards, that the brain has left and right hemispheres, and that each one is (loosely) responsible for different functions. Over the years, education and business have tended to focus on the left hemisphere as being the more 'important' of the two, hailing it as master – of sequential and analytical thinking, number, logic, words etc – whereas the right hemisphere has been regarded as something of the Cinderella of the piece, a poor relation, responsible for simultaneous and contextual thinking, art, music, emotion and so on. Words like 'sensible' and 'structured' tend to be used in connection with the left hemisphere, while 'arty', 'fluffy' and 'soft' are commonplace in the description of the right-brain functions.

And yet psychologists and neuroscientists are now coming round to the way of thinking that, particularly in the conceptual world of the 21st century that Pink describes, both hemispheres are of equal importance in the thinking and learning processes; they don't need to work exclusively of each other. In order to survive and thrive, we actually need both hemispheres to work together, the notion being that the functioning of the whole brain is significantly greater than the sum of its parts. In particular, we need the frontal lobes to be working to their optimal level, these being the part of the brain responsible for what are sometimes called the 'executive' or 'higher cognitive' functions, such as problem solving, empathy, emotions and decision making. Psychologists Greenberg, Williams and Baker (2007) describe this area as the 'crowning achievement in the evolution of the nervous system ... it frees us from routine and leads us into civility, virtue, creativity and innovation' – a goal best achieved when our nervous systems and emotions are in balance. Some of the core principles of whole-brain learning state that:

1. The search for meaning comes through patterning.
2. Emotions are critical to learning and memory.
3. Learning is enhanced by challenge and inhibited by threat.
4. Learning involves both conscious and unconscious processes.

Adapted from www.funderstanding.com

How does storytelling help the learning process?

To answer this question it might be useful to first cast your mind back and reflect for a moment on your favourite stories from childhood ... a recent BBC poll of favourite bedtime stories included *Winnie the Pooh*, *Charlie and the Chocolate Factory*, *The Lion, the Witch and the Wardrobe* and *The Gruffalo* among the top ten. You might include others in your personal collection – the tale of Beowulf or that of Bluebeard, the story of Hiawatha, or the Harry Potter stories. But, whatever your personal preferences, it is interesting to consider, from a learning point of view, what these stories have in common.

In some cases, unless you have young children, you may not have read or indeed thought about these stories for a long, long time. And yet, if I asked you, you could probably recount your favourite tale, almost word for word. I wonder if the same can be said of emails and text messages? Will we be saying to each other, in 20 years' time, 'Gosh, I'll never forget that email you sent me back in 2010!' Personally I doubt it. So we know that one thing all these stories have in common over other forms of communication is that they are memorable – they lodge in the long-term memory long after the daily emails or texts have been deleted and forgotten. American psychologist Jerome Bruner (1990), who investigated different modes of thinking in children, coined the phrase 'narrative thinking', meaning the mind's aptitude to engage in sequential, action-orientated thought. He records that we are some 20 times more likely to remember information in the form of a story than as a set of disconnected facts. So, as trainers, if we want our messages to be remembered long after the training session (and which of us doesn't?), we need to understand more about this particular form of communication. As Rudyard Kipling said, 'If history were taught in the form of stories, it would never be forgotten.'

The search for meaning comes through patterning

Another area common to all stories is that which defines them as a story. For a story to qualify as such, it must comply with what is known as the 'story map' or template. In other words:

- Once upon a time – the beginning.
- And then one day – something happens to make a story.
- The turning point – the crisis, conflict or challenge.
- Happy ever after – some resolution, moral and learning opportunity.

Whether the story is a traditional tale like those above, the latest celebrity scandal you read in your daily paper, or your project team's recounting of how they went about solving a particular problem, the format is the same: we come across the hero or heroine in an ongoing situation, something then happens that changes the status quo, there is some challenge to be addressed – a foe to be fought or a prize to be gained – and finally there is a resolution to this conflict – not necessarily a happy ending in the conventional sense – which very often brings the hero or heroine back to where they started in the story (but naturally a little older or wiser or richer). Conflict in storytelling is not seen as a negative concept – it is just a natural part of the process, and indeed necessary if there is to be a story to tell.

Of course, there are always exceptions to the rule: Ernest Hemingway once claimed that his best 'story' was written in six words: 'For sale: baby shoes, never worn'. E M Forster is quoted as saying that 'The king died and then the queen died' is just a fact, whereas 'The king died and then the queen died of grief' is a story. Neither example conforms to the universal template given above, but the stories are implicit in the spaces between the words. And what is fascinating is the capacity our brains have to fill those spaces. I have never read either of those examples to a group without prompting a sympathetic reaction from the audience. What creates the reaction is of course not just the six or seven words themselves, but the working of our imaginations and internal dialogue mechanisms, which make up their own context for the story and produce an emotional connection to that imagined narrative.

The process of storytelling (and story listening) should not be under-estimated as a learning activity – to engage in it is actually a complex human activity that requires and encourages whole-brain functioning: the left brain is the pattern seeker, the side of the brain that processes the language sequentially, that spots the story map, looks for repetition (one of the fundamentals of storytelling skills), analyses character and plot and registers the archetypal characters (more of them in Chapter 2) that appear in the story. In simple terms the left brain focuses on the 'what' or the content of the story. The right brain, on the other hand, focuses on 'how' and 'why' – it puts all of this information into context, like a jigsaw puzzle; it processes the big picture and visualizes the scene – without which the individual words would be meaningless. The right brain lifts us out of our habitual thinking mode; it is responsible for the comprehension of metaphor and, most importantly, it informs us of how the story relates to us.

Emotions are critical to learning and memory

No tears in the writer, no tears in the reader. No surprise for the writer, no surprise for the reader.

Robert Frost

It may almost sound like a contradiction of the last point about patterns but an incident can lodge in our memory banks when it *doesn't* fit a conventional or recognized model. Since our brains couldn't possibly cope with all the incoming stimuli that it meets during the course of a day, it sifts out the information it perceives as less critical to our survival. Any input that is seen as novel, unexpected or of different emotional intensity to the norm immediately gets our attention – and stories and metaphors excel at this phenomenon. In fact, the crucial difference between plain text and a story is the involvement of the emotions – humour, sadness, anger, curiosity (the point that E M Forster was making). And of course we have the original storytellers to thank for the evolution of narrative in this way. Their role – one of carrying information from one community to another – was of course conducted without the help of the written word; and as such they found themselves faced with two problems:

1. They had to find a way to memorize the information they were given in order to relay it faithfully to their audiences.
2. They had to find a way to recount that information in a way that their audiences would find interesting and memorable.

The storytellers found (purely by chance, as with most good ideas) that the more vivid, colourful and bizarre the imagery they included in their storytelling, the more easily they could remember the information themselves, and the more readily it was taken in and remembered by their listeners. Hence the creation of talking animals, wicked witches and fantasy creatures like giants, wizards and trolls. 'Hello...' says our brain, 'that's not quite right.' And for a short while there is some confusion and curiosity and even destablization in our thinking until we start to assimilate and adjust to the new image.

The reactions to the exercise below are an interesting demonstration of this; I usually find that the group initially resists – 'You can't say that' being a commonly heard comment, or 'That doesn't make sense' – and yet, once it has been explained and accepted that it's all right to break the rules, the imaginations really start to work.

Learning activity

Have 20–30 cards printed in two different colours, with an even mixture of random nouns and similes. For example: **nouns**: a sausage, a smile, fluff, a smell, a tattoo; **similes**: as soothing as, as exciting as, as frantic as.

Ask participants to draw out and read aloud random cards – first a simile followed by a noun, so you could end up with something like: 'As frantic as fluff', 'As soothing as a smile'.

Our learning brains respond well to feelings of curiosity and interest – our metaphorical ears prick up – and indeed many whole-brain and accelerated-learning experts advocate the positive use of curiosity to stimulate learning. Rossing and Long (1981) were among the first to quantify the relationship between curiosity and learning in adults. Their research indicated that curiosity was indeed an important factor in adult learning, because of the perceived value of the information to the learner, and that this was a facet of learning that did not, contrary to popular belief, diminish with age. In storytelling terms, it is easy to see this concept in action: irrespective of what potentially dry topic you may be discussing, you are guaranteed to gain your audience's attention by using such story openings as:

'Don't tell anyone else but...'

'I don't know if you know this but...'

'Have you heard...?'

'You'll never guess what happened when...'

Storyteller Betty Rosen writes: 'I launched into this tale in the tone of voice of one in the throes of sharing secrets of juicy bits of gossip' (Rosen, 1988). But of course, not all stories, and certainly not all storytellers, are naturally riveting – it requires skill and effort (more tips are offered in Chapter 4). Storytelling is definitely becoming more accepted into the business community, but if the method is used unskilfully, there is a real danger of it being seen as just another cliché in the trainer's or coach's portfolio. For stories to have the desired effect, they first have to contain a perceived relevance to the listener, even if tenuous, plus some of the elements that trigger our emotions and challenge or shake up our current values and beliefs – excitement, surprise, conflict, danger, an unexpected event, a strange character, a twist or turn in the plot. Stories have a unique capacity to combine the ordinary with the extraordinary, the mundane with the bizarre, that appeals to and stimulates whole-brain activity. Stephen Denning, author of *The Secret Language of Leadership* (2007), says:

> Stories derive their power from a violation of the normal and the legitimate and the ordinary, which in turn generates the fear and curiosity and excitement which we all feel when listening to a good new story. In this way, stories appeal not only to the mental process of the brain, but are grounded in the feelings of the listener. They thus appeal to both the mind and the heart.

Learning is enhanced by challenge and inhibited by threat

As trainers we need to have the sensitivity to understand what might be perceived as a positive challenge to our learners, and what might generate fear or apprehension. The brain actually operates differently when any type of threat is detected – real or imagined. It uses less of the sophisticated frontal-lobe executive thinking mentioned previously, and resorts instead to using basic survival-type thinking that comes from the reptilian brain stem area. And when this happens, people's capacity for learning, understanding and creative thinking drops like a stone. In this situation it is futile to think we can order people to learn or force them to think creatively.

Hearing information in a narrative format actually changes our brain activity; research has shown that, while listening to stories, or thinking metaphorically, biochemical changes take place in the brain: levels of cortisol (the stress hormone) drop and levels of immunoglobulin A rise – in other words, listening to a story can actually promote relaxation and reduce stress. And stories can help to reduce our brainwave levels from Beta – the wide-awake, fully conscious mind – to Alpha – the state of relaxed awareness. This in turn helps us to bypass our normal, analytical functions; we actually become less critical and more receptive to change and new ideas.

The use of story-based activities provides the relaxed, Alpha state required for learning and yet at the same time, through skilful questioning, the right degree of challenge to stimulate reflective thinking. In Part 2 of this book, you will find two activity sections that follow each story – 'Reflection' and 'Talking points', which are designed to help you put the story into the business context and maximize their use as a challenging and productive learning tool. The sections draw on some of the reflective-thinking models developed by Borton (1970), Gibbs (1988), Kolb (1985) and others, the purpose here being to consider:

- 'What?' (What is the message of the story?)
- 'So what?' (Does it mean anything to me? Can I relate to this?)
- 'Now what?' (What can I do with this additional knowledge or understanding?)

Learning involves both conscious and unconscious processes

Whereas Beta, the 'active' level of brain activity mentioned above, is fine for getting us through the day, it can restrict access to the deeper levels of our mind, ie the unconscious. Some researchers suggest that as much as 99 per cent of learning happens at below conscious level – in other words, learning is going on all the time, not just during a training session and not just when the trainer is talking. Many signals peripherally perceived actually enter our brains without our conscious awareness and interact on unconscious levels. Learners remember what they experience – not just what they are told. Researcher Csikszentkihalyi (1990) suggests that, in order to encourage learning to take place, there are optimal states to be achieved for the learner:

1. High challenge – the learner feels sufficiently motivated and the learning is seen as worthwhile.
2. Low stress – in a relaxed state of mind for learning.
3. Immersed – complete absorption in the event, to the exclusion of other stimuli.

When we listen to a story that is told well, we find ourselves totally engrossed and immersed in the content, in a semi-hypnotic state of mind that psychologists call 'narrative transport' – we can feel real feelings of sadness, joy or outrage depending on the nature of the story; we can relate to the protagonist, either wishing them well or hoping that they come to a sticky end, depending on whether they are the hero or villain.

Metaphor: the key to the unconscious

If a picture is worth a thousand words, a metaphor is worth a thousand pictures.

Lakoff and Johnson, 1980

A metaphor is a comparison, a parallel between two sometimes seemingly unrelated terms. Sometimes it may be purely a literary device, but when used in a learning context (either in training or coaching) a metaphor can be a powerful and innovative way of describing a situation, experience or problem, one that can offer alternative information, help the listener to 're-frame' or see that situation in a different light, and provide them with additional – and sometimes novel – ways of resolving it.

We all use metaphors quite naturally and unconsciously; they are present not just in our everyday speech but also in our thoughts and actions. What metaphors we choose to use to describe ourselves will have a profound effect on how we develop our own model or map of the world. For example, if someone sees life as a battle, they don't just talk about things in that way – they actually live their lives in accordance with that model; they expect conflict, they try to beat the opposition, they work on the premise that if someone wins, another loses. A senior manager I coached described what he judged to be his own outstanding performance during a difficult meeting: 'I just fired a warning shot across his bows ... and I came out victorious...' One wonders if his colleague had the same experience.

For a trainer or coach, the metaphor is a powerful device to promote understanding, to aid clarity, to encourage learning and change and to provide 'compactness' ie the use of a metaphor can offer a sort of shorthand and jointly owned language between you and the learner/s. It is also a powerful agent for change in that unconscious levels of thought are being activated in which there is less resistance and opposition to new ideas.

But it is important to recognize that in the context of learning and change there is no such thing as a universal metaphor. What makes sense to one person will just not 'fit' with another – and worse, could actually offend. Your choice of metaphor must reflect your learners' culture, knowledge, language, frame of reference etc. An HR manager told me recently of the time when a well-meaning colleague, attempting to clarify an issue for her by using a metaphor asked her, 'Do you follow football?' to which she had replied quite candidly, 'No.' Undaunted (and presumably unheeding), his follow-on remark was, 'Well, it's like a game of football...' Such insensitive use of metaphor serves no purpose at all for the learner. And yet exactly the same topic metaphor was used by trainer Roger Greenaway in the UK to great effect in a training session he ran on giving feedback. He says:

> A group of apprentices were talking a lot about football. Perhaps they under-stood the world of football better than any other. So I used their interest in football and their knowledge of the game for setting up and managing a feedback session. The starting point was to identify the skills and qualities needed for different positions on the field of play. Then they had to place each other (physically) on the field of play, giving reasons why they were suited to a particular position... Once they got going, the quality of feedback was surprisingly sophisticated – much more so than if I had asked them to give straight feedback to each other.
>
> *http://reviewing.co.uk/articles/reviewing-for-different-ages.htm*

Choosing the 'right' metaphor for learning and change

If you choose to introduce a metaphor with a coachee or learning group, the participant/s should be able to identify just enough similarity between their situation and that of the metaphor to be able to relate to it, but not so much similarity as to dismiss it as being too obvious or overt – learners quickly see through a story or metaphor if they think there is a hidden criticism lurking in it.

A safer ploy initially can be to listen first to the language used by the individual (if in a coaching session) or by members of groups during discussion, and work with their metaphor rather than introduce one of your own. I coached a senior sales executive who was having problems with a very domineering member of his team. He introduced the metaphor of a jelly, which to him described the problem he was facing: 'This person could be marginally contained, like in a jelly mould, but not nailed to a wall, or micro-managed.' Not only did the use of metaphor give the sales executive more confidence to deal with a difficult, ongoing situation but it added some much needed humour and light-heartedness to what had become a very heavy subject – and provided us both with a quick reference point for future coaching sessions (eg 'What state is the jelly in today?!').

The transcript below is of some coaching work I carried out with another manager working in the medical research industry, who had been given feedback that his leadership style was too autocratic. He was very sensitive and emotional about the subject and initially found it too painful to articulate. He introduced the metaphorical concept of the jigsaw:

Q. When you're aware of this problem, what's it like?

A. It's like a jigsaw with a missing piece.

Q. Tell me about the jigsaw – does it have a shape?

A. Yes – it's round.

Q. And does it have a colour?

A. Not really ... it's black.

Q. And where's the missing piece?

A. It's right in the middle – it's a *big* piece. (gestures)

In this instance the coachee found it much less painful to articulate his feelings using the metaphorical language of the jigsaw and we were able to work on the necessary changes using this method. Be sure not to impose your own perceptions on someone else's metaphor – in this instance it would have been easy for me to interject with 'Can you see the corners of the jigsaw?' – which of course would have been completely incomprehensible to this coachee. It's also important for the trainer or coach to appreciate that it matters little whether you actually understand the metaphor or not – if it makes sense to the person describing it, then you don't need to know the meaning; you are working with process, not content, here.

If you want to use metaphor in this way to encourage learning and change, your role is to help the learner/s to 'unpack' the metaphor using probing statements and questions such as:

Describe...?

When is...?

Where is...?

How many are there?

Who, what...?

What do you see ... hear ... feel?

And if you feel it appropriate, you can attempt a 're-frame'. This is where you try introducing a new or slightly revised metaphor that may help the learner/s to see a situation from a different point of view. So in the jigsaw example above, we could suggest:

What if...?

What if the jigsaw were a different shape?

What if the jigsaw were a different colour?

What would have to happen for the piece in the middle to shrink in size?

Is there a picture on the jigsaw?

Interestingly, after the jigsaw had first been described in some detail, the coachee turned to me and almost semi-accusingly said, 'Where on earth did all that come from?' The simple answer is, of course, 'Your unconscious mind.' We went on to explore how he might reduce the size of the missing piece, and over subsequent weeks the piece got smaller and the jigsaw became brighter – until the final session:

Q. And how's the missing piece?

A. (smiling) I hadn't thought about it until now – it's not really there any more. The jigsaw is like a brightly coloured kaleidoscope with all the pieces fitting in together.

The limitations of metaphors

As trainers or coaches we should also be aware that using metaphors in a learning context does not provide us with a universal panacea. From my experience not all participants 'get' metaphor. In fact, some have actively expressed a loathing of such 'nonsense', preferring to deal with issues in a conventional, linear and left-brain way. Your decision is then whether it is worth persevering – in which case you have to find a skilful way of introducing the concept of metaphor, which is essentially a right-brain methodology, in a left-brain way – or simply introducing an alternative method.

We also need to be aware that metaphors provide us with 'one-sided' insights. Gareth Morgan, in *Images of Organization* (1997), warns that: 'Metaphor stretches imagination in a way that can create powerful insights, but at the risk of distortion.' In other words, the way that metaphor works is that we are encouraged to see the similarities between objects; but, in doing so, we ignore or suppress the differences. If my coachee above sees his problematic leadership style in the shape of a jigsaw, his thinking is being directed in a certain way, ie with a jigsaw-like focus, but it glosses over the fact that his problem might also be a garden, a tangled web, a game of chess or a football. Lakoff and Johnson (1980) suggest:

> To operate only in terms of a consistent set of metaphors is to hide many aspects of reality. Successful functioning in our daily lives seems to require a constant shifting of metaphors.

So we would be well advised to have a range of metaphors up our metaphorical sleeves. The most common 'source domains', ie the concepts that are used metaphorically to provide understanding, tend to come from the categories shown in Table 1.1.

Table 1.1 Metaphor source domains

Source domain	Example
Human body	The *heart* of the matter
Journeys and travel	We're going in the *right direction*
Games and sport	He's got to *first base*
Health and illness	We're living in a *sick* society
Animals	He's a *sly fox*
Buildings and construction	We've laid a *firm foundation*
Machines and computers	She's *hard-wired* to think that way
Movement and direction	Inflation is *soaring*
The elements – heat, light, cold etc	Let's give her a *warm* welcome

To sum up...

- Trainers and coaches have to adapt to the demands of today's organization and maximize the use of informal methods of learning.
- Knowledge sharing through storytelling can be encouraged through 'best and worst' and 'Talking points'-type activities. Avoid saying 'Tell me a story.'
- Storytelling is a form of whole-brain learning that capitalizes on the use of both left and right hemispheres of the brain.
- Stories contain patterns and templates that help the learning process.
- Stories make use of vivid imagery that triggers the emotions and consequently aids learning and memory.
- Learning is enhanced by challenge and inhibited by threat – evidence has shown that listening to a story reduces the level of brain activity, while skilful questioning can provide sufficient challenge to stimulate creative thinking.
- Learning involves both conscious and unconscious processes – and stories and metaphors provide a powerful key to the unconscious.
- You should choose the most appropriate and helpful metaphors for your learner/s – ones that relate to their map of the world, not just yours.
- Be aware that metaphors have limitations: not all learners respond well to them.
- Metaphors provide 'one-sided' insights and distortions.

2

How stories influence

'Thou shalt not' is soon forgotten, but 'Once upon a time' lasts forever.

Philip Pullman

Why do we tell stories?

Not an easy question to answer. On the surface level we might say that telling and listening to stories simply entertain, educate and soothe us. But at a deeper level, there is a strong (and growing) argument to suggest that our brains are actually 'hard-wired' in such a way that makes us process and receive information in a story format more easily than any other form. Where did this thinking originate?

In the 19th century, Adolf Bastian, German ethnologist, introduced the concept of the 'psychic unity of mankind' – the idea that all humans share a basic mental framework. This in turn influenced the likes of psychologists Sigmund Freud (1856–1939) and Carl Jung (1875–1961), both of whom maintained that, just in the same way as human beings are genetically programmed to develop physically, at a deep level we all have the same psychological make-up or structure. They also said that a huge amount of our mental activity went on at a level below our conscious awareness, and their explanation of – and fascination with – dreams, was the way in which the subconscious transmitted messages to the conscious mind.

Jung, as well as studying the importance of dreams, went further in his exploration of the idea of 'archetypes' – models or templates of people or behaviour, which exist in our subconscious and dictate and give meaning to our conscious lives. He said that when we dream, we do so incorporating certain symbols, images and motifs that represent the archetypal patterns in our subconscious. He gave them labels such as:

- The hero – who pursues a great quest to realize his destiny.
- The self – the personality striving towards its own complete realization.
- The shadow – the darker or animal side of humanity.
- The anima – feminine energy.
- The animus – masculine energy.
- The child – the innocent.
- The sage – wise person who has profound knowledge.

He also found that these same archetypes or templates existed in many ancient myths, folk and fairy tales. For example, characters such as these are easily recognizable in traditional stories – such as *The Odyssey* or *Beowulf, Jack and the Beanstalk* or *Little Red Riding Hood*. And interestingly, they are still present today in more modern tales like *The Da Vinci Code*, *Lord of the Rings* and *Avatar*. Indeed, there are those – author Christopher Booker being one – who argue that there are only seven basic plots to all stories throughout the world and throughout time:

> There is in fact no kind of story ... which does not ultimately spring from the same source: which is not shaped by the same archetypal rules and spun from the same universal language.
>
> *Booker, 2004*

Although Jung identified the similarities between dreams and stories, in that they originate from the same source, in more recent times academics like Joseph Campbell and Bruno Bettelheim have pointed out that there are also differences. Although we might be aware of the existence of these archetypes in our dreams, we have no control over the drama that unfolds, and many times our dreams don't have a happy ending – in fact, they often don't 'end' at all, if we're woken prematurely. But in a story, while our unconscious mind relates to these universally recognized symbolic characters, our conscious mind has more of a feeling of controlling the pattern of events. Bruno Bettelheim, in *The Uses of Enchantment* (1991), says:

> Dreams are the result of inner pressures which have found no relief ... the fairy tale does the opposite: it projects the relief of all pressures and not only

offers ways to solve problems but promises that a 'happy' solution will be found.

So hearing a story can lend an optimistic note to a problem or issue that a dream cannot do; a story tells the listener to be hopeful and things will get better; a dream can leave us feeling unsettled and confused. Another difference between the two is in the fact that the archetypes that appear in our dreams are what Joseph Campbell calls 'personalized myth', in other words, they are very often triggered by what is uniquely going on in our lives at a particular time, whereas a story can be accessible to all:

> In the dream, the forms are quirked by the peculiar troubles of the dreamer, whereas in myth the problems and solutions shown are directly valid for all mankind.
>
> *Campbell, 1993*

While the recounting of our own dreams may make no logical sense at all to those we might share them with (sometimes they seem to make no sense to our own conscious minds either) the telling of a story has a universal appeal that all those who listen can relate to in some way and at some level – conscious and unconscious. More recently, writers like Booker have continued to explore this idea, and the accessibility of story as opposed to dreams:

> The archetypal patterns which shape stories provide us with a much more structured picture of the components of the human unconscious than we can derive from dreams. They show us how all the archetypes fit together as part of a dynamic process.
>
> *Booker, 2004*

The identification of these universal patterns might go some way to answering the perennial question posed among story-folk as to why so many similar stories have appeared all over the world, long before the days of global travel and communication. Folklorists report that there are some 1,000 versions of 'Cinderella' that have been floating around since her apparent birth as Yeh-Shen in China in the 9th century (which is one explanation for the emphasis on small feet), and although she might appear later on as Cendrillon in France, Aschenputtel in Germany and Chujo-hime in Japan, the basic template or archetype of the story is the same: the innocent girl (the child), with the help of the beneficent fairy godmother (the sage or earth mother), triumphs over her wicked stepmother (the shadow) to win the hand of the handsome prince (the hero).

So stories have the unique capability of communicating to us using a universal language of symbols that transcends time and culture and operates in our unconscious minds while simultaneously occupying our conscious minds. Stories can cut through the sometimes resistant layer of the conscious mind, which is one of the qualities that make them so effective as a tool for influence and change.

How stories influenced us as children and still do today

The original fairy tales, myths and fables, far from being the rather sanitized cartoon versions that children are sometimes exposed to these days, served a more serious purpose – namely to teach children that life could be tough (unwanted children did actually get led out into the wood and dumped), to expect difficulties and obstacles along the way, and to learn the best way of dealing with them. Many traditional tales speak of great courage, and show that if you're prepared to rise to the challenge, you can overcome the obstacles and emerge victorious.

Stories have always been used as teaching tools – they were used to instruct us in moral codes and values such as integrity, honesty and selflessness. And although some of the relevance of these values or perceived virtues may have changed over time, the effectiveness of storytelling as a tool for influence remains unchanged. For example, 'Pandora's box', the well-known Greek myth, was originally told to caution women against being too curious and daring to question their husbands' actions or motives (however strange). Although this particular lesson would certainly not be acceptable in today's world of equality, the 'happy ending' of the story, forgotten by some, which is that, despite all the problems of the world, we always have hope, is a timeless message.

There is no doubt that the stories we hear as children have a great influence on us; the core values that we learnt from those stories tend to stay with us well into our adult life. Many participants I have met on training workshops have recounted the stories they remember from childhood and how those stories continued to influence them (albeit subconsciously) and the way they lived their adult lives. For example, the little boy whose favourite story was 'King Midas and the golden touch' grew up to be a successful investment manager. The young woman whose mother died when she was young, and whose father remarried the stereotypically uncaring stepmother, saw herself (and lived her life) as Cinderella. The coach/trainer whose main passion was working with clarity and integrity in business cited 'The Emperor's new clothes' as being a powerful influence.

So stories can shape the pattern of and add meaning to our adult lives; equally, reflecting on the stories you remember as a child is a helpful yet simple exercise in identifying your core values and bringing them into consciousness.

Learning activity

Working with a learning partner, identify the stories that you remember most from your childhood – they might be a favourite tale, myth, or fable, an often-told bedtime story, a comic or magazine, a television or radio programme – and ponder the following:

- Why do you remember the story?
- What values, principles or morals did the story reveal to you?
- In what way are you still living these values today?

There is also evidence to suggest that, even as children, hearing a story being told rather than reading it privately would always carry more weight in terms of the effect on the listener. The parent, teacher or relative who told the story would be seen as endorsing and giving credence to the moral or suggested actions of the tale, rather than being only a faceless, unknown author. And the same is true in organizational storytelling: when we (as trainer, coach or manager) tell a story to a group, we are seen as endorsing the underlying values and are naturally associated with them. This is why the choice of story in a modern learning context is crucial and your telling must be seen as authentic – even if the story itself is not your own personal experience. Reading a story alone can be an isolating experience; whereas hearing a story while with others has a bonding effect. I have used many story-based activities as part of team away days, and found an added long-term benefit in that participants derive a common language from the story that keeps going long after the away day has ended.

Story versus facts and figures

Tell me a fact and I'll learn. Tell me a truth and I'll believe. But tell me a story and it will live in my heart forever.

Indian proverb

A couple of months ago I attended a presentation on... well, I think it was something to do with innovative leadership, but more than that I couldn't really say, because I actually can't remember any of it. The presentation was delivered very crisply by a young woman, whose style of presenting was to talk around a never-ending number of slides, on which were listed a large number of supposedly impressive facts, figures and percentages. When I started to think about the presentation the following day, apart from there being one section where the percentages 49 per cent and 51 per cent were mentioned as significant (I remembered them because I wanted to see if they added up) I found I couldn't remember a great deal else of the content. It had clearly been important to the person delivering it, but not necessarily important to the audience she was attempting to influence.

Strangely, I do remember the chap sitting next to me in the audience, who started to tell me (before the presentation began) about his role as a freelance business consultant, how he was passionate about helping small businesses to grow, and how he was having a particular problem with one small company where the people didn't understand what he was trying to do in order to encourage growth. He lamented his own lack of people skills in getting across the message in a way that was acceptable to them.

I later marked these two seemingly trivial incidents as quite enlightening – and not unconnected. Both parties seemed to be lacking something – the first in the style of delivery and the second in the self-reported lack of connection with others. Both people had an important message that they wanted to convey. But only one of them gave me the information in the form of a story that I could relate to and was interested in – and significantly, that was the incident that I remembered. Quite possibly that was also the missing link for both of them in their attempt to connect and influence others.

Earlier this year I ran a storytelling masterclass for a group of senior managers in a retail organization. About 10 days before the workshop, I e-mailed a 'trailer' to the participants, asking them, among other things, to ponder on these two pieces of text:

Read and reflect on these two stories

Recent research carried out in Australia asked people to rate their awareness of positive and negative stories in organizational life. Interestingly, the trend was that people were generally more aware of negative stories than positive ones, with 24.1 per cent of people saying they were aware to a considerable extent of positive stories, as opposed to 41.5 per cent who claimed a similar awareness of negative stories.

Whenever I look at the ring, it makes me smile. I bought it in San Francisco to reward myself for a job well done. The last evening I was there, I dressed up in all my finery, including the ring, hired a limo and went to the theatre. The driver said he thought I looked like the sort of woman who should always ride in a limo. At least, I think that was what he said – he was so far away from me, he could have been saying anything!

On the day, I reminded them of the trailer and asked them what, if anything (and without looking at it again), they remembered. Perhaps unsurprisingly, the majority stated that they remembered the second piece far more easily than the first. When asked why, typical comments were that it made them smile, they could picture the person in the limo (whom I later revealed to be me) and it sparked some sort of emotion in them. In other words, the story affected them in a way that the facts and figures didn't, which subsequently triggered a memory.

Does this mean that we can't include facts and figures at all in our presentations and training sessions? I feel every finance person in the land shuddering with fear. No, of course, we must include relevant content, information and reasoned argument. But we need to be aware that these tools alone will not necessarily and automatically influence a person to take action or change their mind, and indeed being bombarded with argument and factual reasoning alone can often result in people digging their heels in even more and convincing themselves of their own opinion.

Storytelling doesn't replace analytical thinking. It supplements it by enabling us to imagine new perspectives and new worlds, and is ideally suited to communicating change and stimulating innovation.

Denning, 2005

Information in the 21st century is cheap; it's so readily available, when we want it – and sometimes when we don't want it. Thanks to the internet and other applications of technology, we have literally worldwide information at our fingertips. But the fact that information is so accessible also devalues it and we find ourselves overwhelmed. So the last thing we need is more fact. What we do need is help in making sense of the facts; putting facts into a framework that is meaningful for us and allows us to assimilate and take action. Annette Simmons, in her book *The Story Factor* (2006), says:

> Bad decisions are rarely made because people don't have all the facts. Bad decisions are made because people ignore the facts, do not understand the facts, or do not give the facts enough importance ... more facts will not help [them] regain perspective. A story will. A story will help [them] figure out what all these facts mean.

The essence of a story is, as Daniel Pink (2008) refers to it, context enriched by emotion. Stories enhance our understanding by encouraging us to see facts as part of a bigger, more colourful picture, a process that is sometimes known as 'concretizing', ie being able to make sense of a possibly complex concept by associating it with a real, concrete example.

If your role is as a product or technical trainer you may be thinking, 'How do I incorporate this technical data into a story format?' I agree it's a challenge, but hopefully the ideas in this book will help you to think through the process – and it's certainly worth the extra effort in terms of the positive and longer-term effects on learners. As the Indian proverb says at the start of this section, 'Tell me a story and it will live in my heart forever.'

An interesting experiment described in the *Scientific American Journal* in 2006 found that labelling information as 'fact' actually encouraged critical analysis on the part of the listener, whereas labelling information as 'fiction' had the opposite effect – it was far more readily believed. I have found many times in the training room that whereas inclusion of the dreaded role-play exercise is very often dismissed as being unrealistic and manufactured (particularly if the participants don't come out of it too well), the same criticism has never been levelled when I tell a story or use a story-based activity – even though clearly the latter, particularly a traditional fairy tale or fable, is completely unrealistic. I think the difference lies in what each purports to be: stories don't pretend to be based in reality, whereas most role-play activities do.

These incidents suggest that people accept ideas more readily when their minds are in 'story-listening' mode rather than analytical/critical.

How to influence, motivate and mobilize using stories

There is no life I know to compare with pure imagination; living there you'll be free, if you truly wish to be.

Gene Wilder, in the film *Willy Wonka and the Chocolate Factory*

Wouldn't life be easy if we could just *tell* people what to do – 'You just need to be a better manager' we could say, or 'I've worked out your problem – you need to increase sales.' But we all know that life isn't that simple, and influencing others to make some sort of change isn't that straightforward. If it were, why could we not just take and act on the advice, 'Don't be greedy'? Why is listening to the story of King Midas and the golden touch so much more powerful?

Last year I had to have an examination on my throat, which required my having to swallow a long metal tube – something which, frankly, I was looking forward to as much as if someone had told me to cut my head off. A well-meaning friend texted me the day before to say, 'Now all you need to do is ... *just* ... *relax*.' Wise words indeed. I texted back, 'Thanks – *how*?' It wasn't that I was lacking in motivation to carry out her suggestion – simply that the fear I was feeling made any thought of relaxation impossible, and sadly her words gave my overactive negative-thinking brain nothing in terms of guidance or instruction to achieve the desired result.

Stories influence through connecting with our emotions

When we listen and can relate to information in the shape of a story or metaphor, our imaginations and emotions are stirred into life; we start to picture the situation and characters in our minds, and, after time, start telling ourselves a secondary, almost parallel story that has unique relevance to us. It is this 'inner narrative', connecting with our emotions, that engages us and mobilizes us into action. The habitual barriers that very often come up when we are asked to make changes in some way aren't as active. And most of this happens in our subconscious – we don't even realize that we have been influenced. As trainers or coaches, we can help this process to take place by subtly incorporating phrases such as:

Can you imagine?

Can you see how...?

What if...?

Just think, if...

Using these types of phrases invites the listener to imagine the future prospect, but allows them to interpret it on their own terms – in other words, they feel that they (not you) have created the future and will therefore own it and protect it. Research carried out by P K Petrova and R B Cialdini (2005) also found that the degree of ease or difficulty in imagining the suggestions made influenced the willingness on the part of the listener to take action. Therefore the easier you can make it for the listener to imagine incorporating change or taking a particular course of action, the more likely they are to accept it. If my well-meaning friend had suggested that I imagine the approaching tube like a floppy liquorice stick being dipped in sherbet, or helped me to picture an exotic scene where I was swinging idly in a hammock and the tube was instead a plastic straw leading directly to a cool glass of piña colada ... this would have provided me with sufficient stimulus to be distracted away from the reality of the situation and mobilized my body into relaxation mode, eg reduced heart rate, regular breathing, etc. (Fortunately, for those who want to know the end of that story, I was anaesthetized to such a degree I never saw or remembered the tube anyway. All that worry for nothing!)

The power of stories lies in their very gentleness

Stories teach us but they don't nag; they offer advice but don't wag a judgemental finger. They are a subtle, non-invasive means of influencing others and affecting change. They simply describe the situation, offer a solution or make suggestions, and then say 'What do you think? You decide what to do.' In a similar way that students of the NLP school might use an 'embedded command' with a group, eg 'You might like to think about this...', in using a story there is apparently nothing to resist and so the listener is far more likely to accept and go along with the underlying (positive) message that is being conveyed.

As a trainer or coach you can't hope to influence someone who thinks you are making them wrong – the number of times I have seen (or reluctantly been involved) in some sort of procedural training or coaching that starts from the premise that 'You're doing it wrong and I will tell you how to do it right' is proof of that. The group will be sure to resist whatever you are telling them – no matter how sound the strategy or reasoning might be. On a larger scale, governments try to influence the public either by punishment and pressure ('You can't do that'), or by guilty coercion ('You should do this because it's good for you'). The effects of both are limited.

It is a far more effective strategy to show empathy with a group, acknowledge and even respect the current situation, and then suggest – through use of story, metaphor or analogy – another way of thinking. This is not exactly a new idea; that well-known management guru Machiavelli (1469–1527) understood the concept. In *The Prince*, written in 1513 but not published until 1532, after his death, he wrote:

> He who desires or attempts to reform the government of a state, and wishes to have it accepted, must at least retain the semblance of the old forms so that it may seem to the people that there has been no change...

The use of a well-chosen story does not dismiss all that the group has held to be true up until now; rather, it encourages a process of firstly integrating new thinking with old thinking, and secondly of 'structurizing', ie building new structures of learning that can be generalized and applied to other areas. If we want to influence change in others, we would be well advised to spend some time in preparation, finding out what has gone before, what previous strategies were in operation, what was deemed important – in other words the 'back story' – so that we don't inadvertently make those previous actions look foolish or encourage our audience to defend their previous decisions so that there is no loss of face. We can elicit this back-story information through using investigative techniques such as 'Learning histories', described in Chapter 3.

Stories bring about change by degrees; they persuade by first meeting the audience in their world, and then gently leading them by the hand so that ultimately you reach a common point of view without invoking any resistance. Robert Cialdini (2007), expert on the 'science of persuasion', describes the process by reminding us of the old adage, 'The best way to ride a horse is in the direction that the horse is going,' and goes on to say:

Simply trying to pull the horse in the desired direction immediately will just wear you out – and you'll probably just upset the horse in the process.

Stories provide us with a 're-frame'

Particularly during difficult times it's easy to get stuck in the same habitual thinking; hopelessness can become a habit. Stories and metaphors can lift an individual or group out of this mindset and invite them to stand back and see things in a different, more positive way, possibly in a way they've never imagined before. Sometimes this might take the form of a simple rationalization process (as in 'The fox and the grapes' story in Part 2), where we are encouraged to deal with a disappointing outcome by convincing ourselves that it wasn't worth having. On other occasions the story might trigger a whole new way of thinking.

Using stories and metaphors to accelerate the physical-healing process is now a well-documented methodology. Dr Grahame Brown, a musculoskeletal specialist at the Royal Orthopaedic Hospital in Birmingham, spares many of his patients the need to have spinal surgery every year simply by 're-framing the negative metaphors that have been unwittingly used by their doctors that can lead to a destructive and self-fulfilling cycle'. He says, 'I tell patients who work in computers that I've examined their hard drive and it's functioning well but that the software is corrupt and needs to be deleted and replaced with a new, more positive programme.' This is a picture that Brown's patients can easily relate to, that provides some humour and light-heartedness in what might be a traumatic situation, and that offers a different way of tackling it.

Some time ago I was asked to coach a young research scientist, whom we'll call Joe, who had lived for most of his life with a crippling shyness that was holding back his progression at work. Below is my account of how I used a story that he was already very familiar with to provide a re-frame for his shyness:

I discovered, almost by chance, that Joe was passionately involved with playing war games; and that he actually identified strongly with two of his favourite characters – Gotrek, a rather fearsome-looking warrior type and a dwarf called Felix, who is Gotrek's 'Rememberer', that is, he has promised to record all of Gotrek's heroic deeds, including his death. It doesn't take Felix long to realize that whoever or whatever kills Gotrek is pretty certain to kill him too. It is therefore in his interest to protect Gotrek as much as he can. During the coaching, we used these two characters as metaphors to explore the two sides of Joe's nature – the bolder, more assertive one and the timid, shy one. What Joe had been attempting to do for a number of years was to fight off the shyness, not realizing that, the more he engaged in this fight, the stronger his 'foe' became. Through using this metaphor, Joe eventually realized that he didn't have to fight the shyness all the time. When he learnt to accept it – as a useful and protective part of himself – it just naturally disappeared.

Stories provide evidence and develop trust

Words! Words! I'm so sick of words! ... Don't talk of stars burning above; if you're in love, show me! Tell me no dreams filled with desire; if you're on fire, *show me*!

Eliza Doolittle in the film My Fair Lady

In 2009 the Institute for Leadership and Management in conjunction with *Management Today* conducted a survey to analyse levels of trust between CEOs, line managers and employees in a cross section of organizations in the UK, the premise being that 'Leadership and trust have a unique relationship. Without one, the other means nothing.' In other words, a leader cannot hope to exert influence on their colleagues unless the latter feel sufficiently relaxed, confident, trusting – and trusted. The findings showed that CEOs had on average a 'trust index score' of 59 (where 0 is absolutely no trust and 100 is complete trust) – and that the trust levels fell consistently the larger the organization, with those in charge of large public sector organizations (of 1,000+ employees) scoring lowest of all.

The report concluded that in order to develop trust, senior managers must first demonstrate their ability as leaders and secondly display high levels of personal integrity. Undoubtedly, consistent examples of behaviour are the most powerful form of building trust. But how do you ensure that your colleagues get the right message? We've all become aware of the negative connotations of 'spin'. Simply telling people how good you are may keep your image going for a short while, in the same way that declaring 'I am honest and trustworthy' on your CV may get you to the first interview stage. But if you want to really convince people of your reliability, it is best not to spread out your wares so openly and directly, as you may simply arouse suspicion and have the opposite effect to the one you intended. Chris Quin, general manager of Gen-i (a subsidiary of Telecom New Zealand) says:

> Statements from management are, by definition, viewed with suspicion. To get past clichés and dig out the real stuff, you need to find the right stories.
>
> *quoted in Silverman, 2006*

So if you have been appointed as a leader of a new group, or been promoted to a senior position, get into the habit of incorporating stories that imply what you feel to be your positive qualities and let your colleagues come to their own conclusion about you. Barack Obama, addressing students in Arlington, Virginia in September 2009, gave a powerful message that skilfully implied a number of personal qualities:

> I know that for many of you, today is the first day of school. And for those of you in kindergarten, or starting middle or high school, it's your first day in a new school, so it's understandable if you're a little nervous ... and no matter what grade you're in, some of you are probably wishing it were still summer, and you could've stayed in bed just a little longer this morning. I know that feeling. When I was young, my family lived in Indonesia for a few years, and my mother didn't have the money to send me where all the American kids went to school. So she decided to teach me extra lessons herself, Monday through Friday – at 4:30 in the morning. Now I wasn't too happy about getting up that early. A lot of times, I'd fall asleep right there at the kitchen table. But whenever I'd complain, my mother would just give me one of those looks and say, 'This is no picnic for me either, buster.'
>
> Now I know it's not always easy to do well in school. I know a lot of you have challenges in your lives right now that can make it hard to focus on your schoolwork. I get it. I know what that's like. My father left my family when I was two years old, and I was raised by a single mother who struggled at times to pay the bills and wasn't always able to give us things the other kids had. There were times when I missed having a father in my life. There were times when I was lonely and felt like I didn't fit in. So I wasn't always as focused as I should have been. I did some things I'm not proud of, and got in more trouble than I

should have. And my life could have easily taken a turn for the worse. But I was fortunate. I got a lot of second chances and had the opportunity to go to college, and law school, and follow my dreams.

So from this extract we can draw the conclusions that Obama:

- came from a poor background;
- had a supportive mother;
- was tenacious and disciplined in his learning;
- studied long hours;
- values education;
- respected and acknowledged his mother's support;
- felt isolated and out of place;
- got into trouble;
- can relate to the students he is addressing;
- worked hard to follow up the opportunities he was given;
- went to law school;
- set himself goals and dreams;
- succeeded in spite of adversity.

Rather than taking a didactic approach of 'I was good in school, so you should be too,' Obama takes time to first build rapport with his audience so that they can relate to him. The speech implies his personal qualities rather than simply telling, or reading out, what would have seemed to them a boring curriculum vitae. We will allow ourselves to be influenced by someone who we think is like us or at least has had similar experiences to ours.

So in order for leaders – and I include trainers and coaches in that description – to build trust, it can be beneficial to develop a personal portfolio of stories (just in your own head is fine) incorporating some of the following:

- Who you are and what you stand for.
- How you discovered this quality.
- Examples of when you have demonstrated this quality.
- A time in your life when this quality was tested.
- A person/event in your life that taught you the importance of this quality.
- A time when you failed against your own standards and decided to never let it happen again.

Stephen Denning (2005) recommends that 'giving them an account of one or more turning points in your existence can enable listeners to get inside your life, to share your life, to go through what you have been through so that they can themselves experience what sort of person you are'. As well as implying your good qualities, people also like to think that their leaders are real and human and that of course means showing fallibility – in the way that Obama admitted to 'getting into trouble'. Robert Cialdini (2007) discovered that:

> Applicants whose CV contained only wholly positive references were invited to fewer interviews than those whose CV first highlighted a weakness or slight limitation before going on to describe positive characteristics.

The quality implied by this approach is: 'I didn't have to tell you about this – therefore you know I'm honest.'

I have often told participants of the time when I was speaking at a conference, trying to be Ms Perfect (first and last attempt) and only gained rapport with the audience when I fell over a table leg and said, as I thought, under my breath, forgetting about the lapel microphone, 'Oh bum!' – which brought an unexpected round of applause from the audience. At the time I thought they were just laughing at my expense, but it was only when I reflected on it afterwards that I realized that what they were applauding was the fact that I had shown my human face; I had told the audience though my actions, 'I'm just like everybody else ... and certainly not perfect.' This sort of self-disclosure not only helps to build rapport but also encourages reciprocal disclosure from your audience.

To sum up...

- Psychologists say that we are 'hard-wired' to received information in the form of a story much more easily than just hearing facts and figures.
- Stories we heard as children influenced us then – and still do today. We derive our values and beliefs from some of the stories we heard.
- Stories don't replace analytical thinking – they supplement it.
- It is easier to remember information in the shape of a story than as simply facts and figures.
- Labelling information as 'fact' encourages critical analysis whereas labelling information as fiction has the opposite effect.

- Stories influence us by connecting with our emotions – it is our inner narrative that engages us and mobilizes us into action.
- Stories are a subtle, non-invasive means of influencing others and effecting change – they effect change by degrees.
- Stories provide evidence and develop trust.
- Rather than openly telling people, use storytelling to imply yours and others' positive qualities.

3

Sharing the story

There have been great societies that did not use the wheel, but there have been no societies that did not tell stories.

Ursula LeGuin

'Careless talk costs lives'

It would be a very thick-skinned or impervious person indeed who could honestly say that they had never heard of, or been affected by, the term 'credit crunch' – and the accompanying stories of doom and gloom that descended on us thick and fast towards the end of 2008 onwards and spread (in some cases along with swine flu) throughout the world, as we entered the worst recession for many years.

But what impact do negativity and gloom-mongering of this sort have on organizational effectiveness? Was the World War Two slogan about careless talk justified? Anthropologists tell us that any community that persistently tells negative and destructive stories about itself, to itself – the 'Ain't it awful here?' syndrome – is likely to find itself in demise. Stories like this can easily become self-fulfilling (To what degree did we talk ourselves into this recession?) – and they are also contagious. Researchers at Indiana University, examining the effects of such dialogue within groups, carried out experiments where consumers were presented with a new product or service to evaluate. As expected, some evaluations were positive and some negative. However, when the researchers revealed to participants whether their peers evaluated the product in a positive or negative light, they found that the opinions of others exerted particularly strong influence on individual attitudes when those opinions were negative. They also found that those with negative opinions of the product were likely to become even more negative if asked to participate in a group discussion.

Organizational stories and their effects

Organizations, no matter what their size or make-up, are a form of community, and like all communities since ancient times, wherever numbers of people have gathered together – whether it be sitting round the camp fire or standing by the water cooler – they have told each other stories. It's a basic human need, and to attempt to stop the flow would be foolish – and in fact impossible. But this doesn't mean that we should deny their existence or be ignorant of their effects. Only today a colleague told me of his managing director's (not uncommon) response to a flurry of negative stories that had been reported to the HR manager in one particular office – 'Get rid of the HR manager, then they'll have no one to moan to.' Sadly, this seems to be missing the point somewhat. As trainers, we shouldn't dismiss or attempt to quash all storytelling that sounds at first hearing unenthusiastic, critical of the organization or goes against the company procedures manual. Some stories that sound negative in tone can actually contain a positive moral and useful learning opportunity if managed properly. David Snowden, former director in the IBM Institute for Knowledge Management says that:

> There is a tendency, reinforced by techniques such as appreciative enquiry to only look for positive stories. While this may be valid in individual counselling it is not in the context of organizational storytelling where the most powerful and useful stories are often negative.
>
> *Snowden, 2000*

But what exactly constitutes a positive or a negative story? How might they be categorized? Does it depend on the teller or the listener? Anthropologist Peg Neuhauser (1993) advises that we differentiate between the style and topic and the outcome or message:

> ## Positive stories
>
> The people who heard the story felt better off for having heard it, learnt something useful, or their organization benefited because the story was told.
>
> ## Negative stories
>
> The people who heard the story felt worse off for having heard it, did not learn anything useful, or their organization was damaged in some way because the story was told.

Interestingly, I find that very few individuals tell truly negative stories against themselves. They can talk endlessly about 'the time I took on the local council / the telecoms company / my mother in law' but always manage to emerge the hero of the piece. It's very rare that someone will admit 'Yes, I was totally to blame on that one.' Gerald Ratner, once head of the jewellery chain, Ratner's, in the UK, is most famously remembered for 'that speech' when he denigrated his own products, declaring them to be 'crap'. The company lost around £500 million as a direct result. Without doubt, Ratner now regrets saying it, and would surely categorize it as a negative story; however, having presumably learnt from his own cautionary tale, he is now making quite a nice supplementary living out of telling the story on the corporate speaking market. So stories themselves are not inherently positive or negative – it depends very much on the context, the teller and the telling, with the emphasis being on the perceptions of the listeners rather than the intentions of the teller.

Storytelling or corporate propaganda?

Stories are the single most powerful weapon in a leader's arsenal.

Howard Gardner, Harvard University

Organizational stories, when monitored and managed, can be a powerful resource for both internal and external communication; they can feature on the company intranet, website, in training sessions and team meetings. But wherever and whenever they are told, if they are to have a positive effect on the listener/s, they must be seen to have relevance and credibility and be in pace with surrounding current events.

In January 2009, while the world was still very much in the grip of recession, UK business minister Baroness Vadera made a speech where she commented that she could see a few 'green shoots' of economic recovery. Unfortunately, the speech was made on a day when many UK firms had announced large-scale job losses and share prices had slumped by almost 5 per cent. The Baroness, rather than being viewed as cautiously optimistic as she had intended, was immediately vilified by colleagues as being insensitive and out of touch with reality.

With the advent of the internet and other social media, there is no shortage of communication methods that can be employed both inside and outside an organization. However, the disadvantage of this plethora of information is that the content itself becomes devalued, and consumers become ever more sceptical of what they see and hear. Every business website (from window cleaners to multinationals) now carries some statement along the lines of 'Our staff are our greatest asset' and 'We are customer focused,' but consumers are beginning to realize that words like this, on their own, are cheap, and are becoming more discerning in seeking out the evidence that supports these claims.

Stories provide social proof

Communication that provides 'social proof', ie stories from genuinely satisfied customers or genuinely engaged members of staff, carry far more weight in terms of gaining the attention of the reader or listener and building trust and confidence, than standard 'copy speak'. This is particularly relevant in an unstable and cynical economy, when customers and employees alike need some form of reassurance.

Last year I was approached by a small fuel company, BDS Fuels (www.bdsfuels.co.uk), to help them elicit some success stories from their customers, with the intention of incorporating them as part of their 'brand narrative', for use on their website, in promotional materials and so on. The managing director particularly wanted to highlight the company's unique selling point, which was that they did not see themselves in competition with the faceless Big Boys in the fuel world, but rather that their strength lay in the fact that they were small, local, and offered a friendly, professional service. I conducted, on the company's behalf, a number of semi-structured telephone inter-views, and from the information I was given, crafted the stories, weaving into each story illustrations of the values the company wanted to highlight. Below is an extract from Mr A's story, one of their more recent customers:

Local family firm

We started looking round for another supplier. When we saw the BDS website, I said to my wife, 'That looks like a local family firm, more like the sort of firm we want to deal with. Let's contact them.' We knew from their attitude straight away, you could tell on the telephone, it was obvious that they were much more caring. The staff in the office were polite, pleasant, they couldn't do enough to help and to explain things for you. Their prices were a lot cheaper than we'd been paying too, and they gave a discount for prompt payment.

'You leave it all to us...'

The switch over went very smoothly. They said, 'You leave it all to us. When you've signed the form, you forget about it. We do it all for you; we contact your last supplier and take care of everything.' And that's just what they did... My wife and I are both pensioners. With the prices we were being charged last winter, we didn't dare put the central heating on. We went to the lengths of buying a log-burning stove and we used electric fires because they were cheaper than LPG. We have no fear now of turning the central heating on and using it as it should be used. I can't speak highly enough of the company. Compared with the big-four suppliers they are a small family firm. But they are exactly the sort of firm that we want to deal with – and will for a long time to come.'

Since the redesign of their website to include the success stories, the fuel company's turnover has risen by approximately 15 per cent. In addition, an unexpected bonus from this story-gathering project was the positive effect that it had on company employees. Being able to read what their customers actually thought of them (but probably had never said) gave them a huge, motivational lift. In addition, it served as a useful learning tool; the staff understood far better what their customers liked and didn't like and were able to focus on meeting those needs. The company's managing director said, 'We had never even considered the potential for creating a feeling of well-being for our customers by using the experiences of others to put the message across. I wish we had done it years ago.'

A similar approach can be taken to internal customer care. I was invited to work with a national heritage centre, teaching their customer-facing staff storytelling skills to enhance the visitor experience. During the course of our group discussions, one of the centre guides told the moving story of a little boy who had visited the centre as part of a school trip. Although he had been the most troublesome of them all during the day – constantly regaling her with cries of 'Miss, what's this, Miss?' 'Can we look at this, Miss?' – at the end of the tour, he had tugged on her sleeve and said, with a somewhat toothless grin, 'Miss, this has been the *best* day of my life!' Not surprisingly, her colleagues were very touched by the tale – and also intrigued. 'I've never heard you talk about that before,' said one of her fellow workers. 'I never thought to tell anybody,' she replied genuinely. Just think how many other wonderful stories like this may be lurking in your organization, just waiting to be told. Casey Hibbard, author of *Stories that Sell* (2009), talks of the power of the customer success story to act as a product or service endorsement:

> Stories help people imagine scenarios and gain inspiration from seeing others' success – and they are moved to act as a result.

We can see from the two examples given above that stories can be just as effective if used for internal or external marketing purposes. If given the choice, most of us would generally rather listen to, and take heed of, stories and endorsements from our colleagues, friends, or people we trust before deciding what, if any, action to take.

However, like any other organizational initiative, care should be taken if embarking on a story-gathering project. Once (long ago) I inad-vertently chose to highlight a story from a member of staff who, it tran-spired, was known as the most cynical naysayer in the company ... whoops! Although the story she told was a great one (and very motiva-tional) the fact that her colleagues knew that the story was not going to be backed up with her actions meant that the story lost credibility (and I probably did as well, but it was a long time ago!). There is nothing wrong with telling a story where the protagonist demonstrates that they have had a change of heart, or struggled to overcome a challenge; in fact some of the strongest branding stories are those that start with a problem or a negative belief – 'I didn't believe this would change my life,' 'I didn't think you could do it in time,' sort of premise – but they must come from credible sources. One can see the gradual change in trend, certainly in the UK, in television advertising, from the use of professional actors with digitally enhanced gleaming smiles and well-scripted lines to real-life customers or members of an organization. What they lose in acting ability (I have to admit some of the worst ones do have the look of a bad school Nativity play) they gain in authenticity.

If you're considering embarking on a story-gathering initiative, for either internal or external purposes, I would suggest you follow these project guidelines:

1. Decide on the objectives of the programme, who will manage the project, what aspects of the organization you wish to highlight, how you are going to use the stories, in what format, etc.
2. Identify a number of customers/staff who may be suitable. This will depend on the size of your organization, but assume that 30 per cent of those you target will be unsuitable or unavailable.
3. First letter/e-mail goes out to customers or staff, outlining the initiative, asking their permission and offering some incentive. For your customers this may be a special discount on your product/ service; for staff it may be a meal voucher, a paid holiday, etc.
4. Decide and agree on the questions that the interviews will be based on.
5. Conduct telephone or face-to-face interviews and gather information. (If you think it more appropriate, record or video with permission, for use in podcast or video clip on your website.)
6. The information given is crafted into a story (this can either be done in-house if you have the necessary skills, or by an external consultant).
7. Draft stories are given to participants for their approval. Written approval should be given (particularly by external customers) for use to publish in promotional materials. Double-check with them any confidential or sensitive issues.
8. The stories can be showcased on your website, intranet, newsletters, blogs, and can also be used in future sales presentations and for discussion in training, knowledge sharing, focus groups or team meetings.
9. A database should be created to keep records of which stories have been used. Stories that feature on your website should be updated or rotated every three to four months to keep them fresh.

Stories define organizational culture

The stories from our customers and our employees are an inspiration to all of us at Johnson & Johnson, and they're part of why we come to work every day.

www.jnj.com

Organizational culture is one of those nebulous concepts, like oxygen, that we all know exists but nobody can quite put their finger on what or where it is. Understanding the culture that pervades your organization helps to contextualize certain perceptions, attitudes and behaviours; it explains why one group of people performs differently to another and impacts upon people development and ultimately job satisfaction. Developed originally from the school of anthropology, various definitions exist including 'a pattern of basic assumptions' (Schein, 1985) and 'the way we do things round here' (Atkinson, 1990). Johnson (1992) talks of a more complex 'cultural web', which highlights a number of different aspects that typify an organization's culture including: *routines* – the ways members behave towards each other and towards those outside the organization; *symbols* – such as company logos, cars, titles and commonly used language and terminology; and, of course, *stories* – told by members to flag up important events and personalities and typically acknowledge successes, failure, heroes, villains and mavericks.

Stories define the culture of an organization – indeed some might argue that stories *are* the culture. They are certainly a crucial part of the communication process that helps tell the world at large about your organization's identity – 'Who we are', 'What our purpose is', 'What we stand for' and in some cases 'How it all began'. They give an organization a firm foundation and a confident sense of self, as evidenced by healthcare and pharmaceutical company Johnson & Johnson, quoted at the start of this section, who have created a whole database of employee stories for use on their website.

However, it might be argued that storytelling tends to focus on and reinforces the past rather than acknowledging the present or indeed the future – tales of 'the good old days' abound in some companies and are passed from one generation of staff to the next, even though many of them weren't even around to remember the days in question (see 'Monkey business' story in Part 2). So what happens if you want to change the culture? Consultant Peter Bregman, writing in the *Harvard Business Review*, recounts offering this advice to a client:

[Don't] change the performance review system, the rewards packages, the training programs. Don't change anything. Not yet anyway. For now, just change the stories.

blogs.hbr.org/bregman

Listen to, and be on the lookout for, 'story-worthy' incidents that talk of the actions and behaviours that you are trying to nurture in the organization; tell the stories during training and coaching sessions and team meetings; post them on the company intranet if you have one, or circulate via e-mail; encourage others to tell the stories so that more people begin to emulate the behaviour. To encourage the use of stories to help define or redefine your organization's culture, you can consider the following:

- What are the company vision and purpose? Listen to and find stories that illustrate these and retell them, both inside and outside the company.
- Who are the 'tribal elders' of the company? Encourage leaders to relate personal experiences and share lessons learnt from both successes and failures.
- Encourage leaders and managers to make positive storytelling a regular feature in team meetings.
- Retell favourite stories that keep the legacy alive and reinforce the company's core purpose (but don't get stuck on out-of-date stories).
- Be on the lookout for new stories to introduce (particularly as the organization changes).
- When people find a new way of doing things, tell their success story, which will encourage others to follow.
- Coach people in how to use stories with confidence as part of their presentations.
- Elicit stories that focus on the strengths and successes of the company.
- Consider the use of art and technology where appropriate to enhance and spread the stories.

Adapted from Silverman, 2006

Metaphor and culture

New metaphors have the power to create a new reality ... much of cultural change arises from the introduction of new metaphorical concepts and the loss of old ones.

Lakoff and Johnson, 1980

A crucial skill for leaders and managers of today's organizations is to be able to interpret and understand the nature of their organization and what makes it tick, in order to be able to influence it and shape it for the future. And in this context the use of metaphor can be quite illuminating. We use metaphors as part of our day-to-day lexicon – quite naturally referring to a 'rags to riches story', 'the Midas touch' and 'the Goldilocks effect'.

But metaphors can also be used in a more deliberate and systematic way; they can be used as a research tool in determining the state of health of an organization. This does not suggest replacing the information gleaned from conventional attitude surveys; however, in my work with people in organizations I have probably learnt as much (if not more) by listening to the metaphorical language that is used by members and the accompanying behaviours. Some of the more common types are listed in Table 3.1.

Being aware of how members see and describe their organization gives you first a way of establishing and maintaining rapport, ie you can respond to colleagues using the same or a similar type of language, and secondly, it provides a subtle but effective tool for influencing or changing culture. For example, a manufacturing company I worked with some years ago had an extremely aggressive culture: the staff talked mainly in 'battle' language – everything was described in terms of 'winning' and 'losing', 'attacking' opponents, being 'shot down in flames'. Had I attempted to communicate or build rapport with these people by talking of 'nurturing' and 'growth' and 'development', it would have created a huge mismatch of communication. (I didn't dare mention the word 'storytelling'!) However, I can respond by talking of 'effecting a truce' or 'a peace process' or 'a tactical plan' and the language is easily understood and accepted.

Table 3.1 Common metaphors

Source domain	Behaviours	Sayings
Battle	Conflict, competition, struggle, aggression, opposing views	It's a minefield We're warring factions Don't stick your head above the parapet
Garden	Relationships nurtured, developing, growing, producing	We're growing all the time Planting the seeds for the future Nurturing our staff
Journey	Adventure, ambitious, planned progress, travel, exploration	We're at a crossroads This is our destination We're nearly at the finishing line Crossing the bridge
Machine	Routines, projects, schedules, re-engineering	It's going like clockwork A well-oiled machine Keep the wheels turning Who knows the workings of his mind?

Stories to illustrate organizational values

I've lost count of the number of people I've spoken to in organizations who, when asked what their company's values were, either looked completely blank or, with eyes glazed, repeated, automaton-like, a list of grandiose-sounding but apparently meaningless words and/or phrases, among which you could guarantee featured the ever-popular 'We value customer care / innovation / integrity' (or variations on this theme). It would almost be as unthinkable *not* to include such words in a values statement as it would be to conceive of a prospective candidate on a dating site declaring that they had no sense of humour.

I was asked by a construction company some time ago to help them review their company values. Having listed the current values, I asked the group to consider, 'What do those mean to you?' Again, I was greeted with the familiar glazed expression. I explained to them that if your organization is listing 'customer care' as one its key drivers, then surely there must be plenty of evidence in the form of stories and incidents to illustrate and support that claim. Using the story map explained in Chapter 1 as a guide, and some 'story-prompt' questions to get the dialogue flowing, participants were encouraged to reminisce about their work experiences and link those experiences to their organization's values. Although initially it took a while to tease some of the stories out of them, the results were certainly worth waiting for. Not only did the participants come to see for themselves the meaning of their core values and the part that they played in them, but they also developed a new habit of telling positive stories to each other and their customers. The managing director later commented:

> We never told uplifting stories before. We were too quick to focus on where we'd gone wrong. Having introduced this as a regular feature of our team meetings, the team is buzzing. They're all really motivated and, for once, working as a team.

This use of storytelling is an effective means of bringing values to life, and undoubtedly a more effective option than senior managers simply dictating or moralizing to their staff – which you can guarantee is an invitation for resistance. Which of us really likes being told that we must comply and conform without question?

Encouraging the telling of value stories means that the values themselves become more than merely words, and are given a human context that relates to both reason and emotion. Staff become involved and engaged in the process and therefore also feel themselves to be equally involved and connected with the values – indeed you could say that they *become* the values. Another of my clients, a pensions organization, having originally involved all their staff to help identify their values (committed, cost effective, ethical, customer focused, innovative, united), was determined to keep the values alive and meaningful. Last year they launched a Values Awards Ceremony, in which a number of staff were nominated for having best demonstrated one (or more) of the six values, and then the whole organization voted for who they thought to be the most deserving. Below is an example of one of their nomination forms (the form has been slightly amended to protect confidentiality).

Values Awards 2010

Nomination form

Person/s being nominated: Heather

Which category: Customer focus

Reason why this person/team should win an award:

Heather always provides excellent internal and external customer service. She has spent hours on the phone with eBusiness employers helping them to put through their submissions, and has shortly agreed to go to London to help one of our clients with their August submission. When account managers request information, she is always quick to respond.

If deadlines are looming, for example with the cut-off for amendments, Heather will take on extra work in addition to her current projects to ensure that our customer service remains unaffected. Despite a heavy workload, she makes herself available to less-experienced members of the team who all know they can come to her with queries, etc, and she will always bear in mind how something will look to a customer in the answers she provides. She frequently puts herself in the position of the customer when she is looking through things, for example the new website, and if she sees something that she thinks could be improved she will ensure she mentions it to the relevant person.

Nomination submitted by: Laura

Not only did the values awards benefit the individuals and teams concerned, but the whole exercise lifted the values back into the spotlight again for some time to come afterwards – and of course proved a useful learning tool and encouraged others to emulate the examples of their peers.

Managing the grapevine

In some of today's organizations, it seems that the most reliable or consistent form of communication is the one we know as 'the grapevine'. This powerful form of storytelling, whose name originated during the American Civil War to describe the telegraph lines that were strung through the trees, tends to be most active during times of change and stress and when the formal channels of communication are deemed to be ineffective, insufficient or just not speedy enough. It is usually fuelled by uncertainty about the future and is often subversive in tone – so the knee-jerk reaction is to want to quash it. But with the advent of social networking sites like Twitter and Facebook, the grapevine is even easier to maintain, and not so easy to stop. But, like so many other 'naughty' activities we're warned against (like drinking or smoking or overeating), attempts to suppress these naturally occurring stories will only result in the operation going underground and blossoming.

So how do you deal with this phenomenon? You can simply deny all rumours (and we all know how well that has worked in the past with certain sports personalities and politicians). You can compel staff to listen to the official party-line speech – but you can't control how much of this they take in or believe, nor can you control individuals' retelling of the information. People will always refashion stories to fit in with and reinforce their own values and beliefs, so that they can finish the tale with a triumphant 'See, I told you so...' or as my late mother-in-law used to say, with a sage-like and emphatic nod of the head '*Now* then...'

Some alternative and more productive ways of dealing with the grapevine are:

1. Be aware of by whom, where and when any perceived negative or damaging stories are being told.
2. Ask yourself why this person is reacting in this way. Usually it is a form of attention seeking or sympathy pleading. Can you offer them this attention through a more positive route?
3. Don't attempt to force them to stop. Human nature is such that they will want to do it all the more.
4. Empathize without getting sucked into a negative story.
5. Don't automatically discount all negative-sounding stories. They can be very important inasmuch as they give us the opportunity to learn from someone's experience.

6. Find the positive angle to the tale. People very rarely tell stories against themselves. Focus on this aspect and use it for the future.
7. Turn an apparent negative into a positive by saying, 'What do you want instead?' or 'What would be a solution to this problem?' 'Why are you telling this story?' (Avoid saying 'And what did we learn?' It sounds a little trite and dismissive.)
8. Encourage positive storytelling, with 'hero' and 'Didn't we do well' stories.
9. Inject your own 'counter-stories' that in time become part of the grapevine.

Knowledge sharing using storytelling

As we touched on in Chapter 1, story sharing can be a useful form of informal learning. But is this informal style of knowledge acquisition a reliable way of learning? The plus side of story sharing is that it is natural and spontaneous, it is self-directed and therefore presumably highly motivated and relevant to the individuals concerned; the downside is that we cannot always legislate for the quality or the accuracy of the knowledge being relayed to others. The process of instruction we used to refer to as 'sitting by Nellie' presupposes that Nellie has both the knowledge and skills to teach the right thing and the motivation to do it. One of the problems associated with knowledge sharing is the fact that the 'expert' is sometimes unable to articulate their knowledge; the process requires the transfer from tacit knowledge to explicit knowledge and this is where storytelling or use of metaphor can sometimes play a part – they help people to 'express the inexpressible'.

A company website I came across recently had a page containing stories from their graduate recruits, entitled 'A day in the life'. This was a great idea in principle, but, because these young people's writings obviously hadn't been vetted in any way, they consisted mainly of information on what was most important to a young person, eg how awful the day had been, how they managed to pop out at lunchtime for a quick sandwich and couldn't wait till the end of the day, when they were looking forward to a glass of wine. They were honest accounts, of course – but one has to consider the potential readers: is this really the image this company wants to offer to other potential graduate trainees? Better perhaps to conduct interviews (however informal) or at least guide the person whose knowledge you are attempting to gather, in order to obtain a more useful account.

Learning histories

It is often said that experience is the best teacher – but is this true in organizational life? Is there not a tendency to gloss over an organizational gaff or stumble along after a downsizing or merger, oblivious to the mistakes that were made and the potential lessons learnt? And in any case, how would one capture the experiences of busy people in organizations?

One way of dealing with this and encouraging knowledge sharing is in the approach known as 'learning histories', developed by Art Kleiner and George Roth, which draws on the ancient practice of community storytelling (as one might experience sitting round the campfire) and the modern practice of collective learning. The learning history, or jointly told tale, is a written narrative of a company's critical event – a new product, a merger, a corporate change – in the words of many of those involved, each with their own perspective. The narrative is written after a number of reflective interviews are carried out (usually by an outsider) as part of what I call the story-gathering stage. Each person is quoted directly, but identified only by job title, and the report is produced using two columns – on one side, the comments; on the other, commentary offered by the story gatherer, which identifies recurring themes, poses questions and raises the sometimes contentious issues that may possibly have been ignored. How the learning history differs from a conventional consultant's report is that, rather than ending up on a shelf gathering dust (which apparently some 70 per cent of commissioned reports do), it is then used as the basis for ongoing discussion and action, where the comments are debated and any necessary action determined.

I carried out a learning history project with a large manufacturing organization that had undergone a huge corporate change programme, rather mystically named 'Horizon', which, rather than leaving the staff feeling engaged and motivated, had left them traumatized and fearful. The story-gathering interviews, conducted with some 20 members of the organization, including managing director, senior managers, team leaders and administration staff, were all recorded, analysed, then written up as the learning history. The framework for the interviews was loosely categorized into 'Past, Present and Future', and individuals asked to reflect on their feelings about themselves, others and the business as a whole. At the subsequent discussion meeting, which consisted of all those involved in the story-gathering process, a number of comments/questions for debate were suggested; for example:

- What would have to happen for people to start trusting each other again?
- The majority of people thought the future *could* be good; there seems a reluctance to commit, although everyone wants the same thing. Is everyone waiting for someone else to make the first move?

The learning history helped many people to see the way forward, to learn not just from each other's experience but also from their own and each other's fears and concerns, and to believe that change was possible. In general, using storytelling in this way has a number of positive effects:

1. They build trust. People who previously felt unheard or under-valued had an opportunity to express their thoughts and share their knowledge.
2. People are not alone. When the learning history is read and discussed, those who have felt isolated realize that there is maybe more commonality than they thought in terms of what each person – and the business – is trying to achieve.
3. An opportunity for collective reflection and learning. The group discussions help to clear the air, to raise issues that have not been dealt with, which in turn allows a higher level of confidence in one another, and creates an environment more conducive to learning.
4. An opportunity for sharing knowledge. Rather than just copying the lessons others have learnt (which might not be totally appropriate in a different situation), readers of learning histories can discover more about others' reasoning that lay behind a particular decision.

Adapted from Kleiner and Roth, 1997

To sum up...

- Be careful how you categorize positive and negative stories; it depends very much on the context, the teller and the telling, with the emphasis being on the perceptions of the listeners; either type can become self-fulfilling.
- Stories told within the organization need to be reinforced by actions in order to be believed – otherwise they are seen simply as corporate propaganda.
- Social proof, ie eliciting genuine success stories from customers and staff, carries far more weight in terms of credibility than basic 'copy speak'.
- Stories can help to define an organization's culture – be on the lookout for 'Who we are' stories that help to describe purpose and vision.
- Circulate stories that reinforce the culture and values you are trying to nurture.
- Stories bring values to life and give them real meaning.
- Be aware of and learn to manage the grapevine.
- Storytelling can be used for knowledge sharing – but must be managed, however nominally, in order to obtain the most useful results.
- Learning histories are a means of learning from a critical incident in the organization that encourages dialogue and builds trust.

4

Telling the tale

Telling a story is the closest thing we have to magic.

Joanne Harris

Where and when (and when not) to incorporate story into the learning process

Hopefully you're convinced, if you've read the rest of this book, that using stories, metaphors and story-based activities as part of your trainer's toolkit can be a powerful resource to help you achieve your and your learners' outcomes more effectively. When used appropriately, business storytelling can:

- make the learning process more effective, engaging and memorable;
- bring statistics and data to life;
- lend an insight into the health of an organization;
- define organizational culture;
- make organizational vision and values more meaningful and attainable;
- encourage the change process to take place by bypassing conscious resistance;
- develop trust and engagement with customers and staff by providing social proof;
- encourage others to get out of habitual thinking patterns by providing a re-frame;
- encourage reflective, imaginative and productive thinking.

You now have to decide when and where it might be best to use this information. If you're anything like me, you will want to dash off and start using your new-found knowledge straight away. But remember, you are the expert on your own organization: you have to consider whether using storytelling is an appropriate medium in your particular setting and if so, what sort of stories would be best used to support your culture, values and so on.

And storytelling can go wrong. I have heard a number of accounts recently from HR directors of organizations who employed storytellers (without meeting them first) to address a business or leadership conference, and then found themselves having to explain to their horrified delegates the relevance of the person in a brightly coloured jester's outfit, who cheerily sang and danced their way round the conference room. This particular genre of storyteller can be wonderful in the right setting – which is more typically a school, library or community centre with groups of children. Children's storytelling concerns itself more with entertainment; it is a dramatic performance – which is often too theatrical, too 'over-the-top' for the jaded and stressed-out business person and can totally miss the point of what you're trying to achieve. If you're thinking about hiring the services of a storyteller to help you achieve a serious business objective, choose one that has a business or organizational focus and the business experience to back it up. I explain to any potential client that I am a business person first and a storyteller second, meaning that storytelling is, for me, a means to an end, not the end in itself.

If you're planning on tackling the role of storyteller yourself, you also have to be sensitive and responsive to your audience – there is a danger of telling too many stories, or telling the same one so often that it has an adverse effect. Be aware of the feedback (verbal and non-verbal) that you get in response to your '...and that reminds me of another story...'. If you are greeted with the 'rolling eyes' syndrome you know you've overdone it. You will also need to think carefully about whether or not to introduce the term 'storytelling'. In some organizations the negative connotations of the word are such that it simply isn't worth the risk of jeopardizing the success of your initiative – and your confidence. You may deem it more appropriate (and safe) to use phrases like 'business narrative' or 'creative communication'. Better still, don't label it at all. As consultant Mary Grace Ketner advises, 'It's your job to bring story out, not bring it in. You can't impose storytelling on organizations.' I'm sure if given the choice you would much prefer that people focused on the positive results of your chosen learning method rather than on the method itself. The introduction of business storytelling should be a subtle one.

Using stories as part of an induction programme

I always think that induction training is one of the hardest areas a trainer has to deal with. It can be thought of as inherently boring and repetitive to the trainer (particularly if you're carrying out 'mass' inductions, as I used to in the retail sector where there is traditionally a high labour turnover), and yet it is crucial to the new starter, as this is their very first impression of the organization that they have joined.

Many organizations have now realized the importance of induction, designing sophisticated, blended learning approaches that are far more effective. And yet others that I have witnessed, not that long ago, still insist on dragging the poor unfortunate round nameless offices, to meet innumerable and instantly forgettable people.

A better approach might be to bring the process to life by including company stories and storytellers; many of the 'tribal elders' that we mentioned earlier – they are the people who founded your organization or who have been there longer than anyone cares to remember – have some great stories to tell that can really benefit a new recruit. But it's important that you choose your storytellers wisely and give them guidance. I have seen some very well-meaning directors and business owners go off like loose cannons and put the fear of God into an inductee. I would suggest taking a coaching role with your storyteller volunteers, asking such questions as:

- What story are you going you tell? (Guide them into the sort of areas or values of the business you want to highlight.)
- Why are you telling that particular story? (Encourage them to see the relevance of the tale, which will improve its focus and telling.)
- How will the inductee benefit from hearing that story? (Encourage them to see the situation from the other person's point of view – is it positive or negative?)
- What aspect of the organization does this story reinforce? (Possibly how and why the company was founded, its mission or core values.)

At Success Stories, we also work with organizations in helping them develop their own 'Life story'. The process involves our conducting a number of interviews with the tribal elders of the organization, writing up their comments in story or cartoon format, and then illustrating the words, which can then be used in hard copy or posted on a company intranet for use in the induction or knowledge-sharing process. More details are available at www.success-stories.co.uk.

Using stories before a training session

I often send out a 'training trailer' to participants, usually around seven to ten days prior to the workshop, that includes the usual purpose and overview of the training, all the domestic details, plus a short story or snippet or metaphor for participants to reflect on before the day. Below is an extract from a trailer I sent out to participants from a finance organization, with whom I was working on coaching skills.

Before the day...

You may like to ponder this short story and consider what it tells you about change and the coaching process.

Two caterpillars

Two caterpillars were sitting on a cabbage leaf, having a chat. Suddenly they heard a loud swishing noise, and looking up, saw a beautiful butterfly flying overhead. The first caterpillar looked to the other, shook his head and said, 'You'll never get me up in one of those things.'

Margaret Parkin, *Tales for Coaching* (2001)

You can use the same sort of activity just as effectively with individuals prior to a coaching session, by asking them to reflect on a story or metaphor that you can discuss at your next coaching session. I do stress, if you're using any sort of pre-learning activity like this, make sure you reference it during the day. If your participants have taken the trouble to contact you, or at least demonstrated that they have reflected on the story, they need to feel that you have acknowledged their contribution.

Unfinished stories and nested stories

When you become more confident in your storytelling you can experiment with 'nested' or 'embedded' stories, ie starting one story, stopping
somewhere in the middle of it, and then using a transition phrase (like
those mentioned later in this chapter) to start another story. (Scottish
comedian Billy Connolly is a master of this.) Make a mental note of the
stories you start so you remember to close the loops. You might also try
telling the beginning of a story at the start of a training session or
meeting, just enough to whet the appetite to create an open frame, and
then...

Using stories for group discussion

Stories such as 'Nasrudin and the tigers', 'The chess set', 'The goose that
laid the golden eggs', or '*WarGames*' in Part 2 of this book are great
tools to encourage reflective, creative discussion in a training group. In
order to get the most out of them, I would advocate following these
steps for the most productive discussions:

1. Read or paraphrase the story to the group; encourage participants
   to listen.
2. Introduce the questions – keep the participants thinking in story
   mode.
3. Give out scripts – to those who ask.
4. Finally, relate the story back to your organization and the issue in
   hand. Help them to make the links.

In more detail, these steps are:

1. You read or paraphrase the story first, before you give out any
   handout or script. At this point you are encouraging the right brain
   to activate, and if participants begin reading the text themselves it is
   the left brain that is in operation. You want them to focus on the
   story and your storytelling, and allow the imaginative process to
   kick in.
2. After the reading, I tend to allow just a few seconds for the story to
   sink in, and then lead into the questions I want the group to address.
   Sometimes you find that participants begin discussing even before

you have asked any questions – so much the better. Your role during this exercise is to encourage the groups to stay in story mode if possible, ie discussing the characters in the story rather than launching straight into a mundane or everyday debate. This ensures the continuation of whole-brain activity.

3. Not everyone wants or needs to see a copy of the story – it tends to be the visual or kinaesthetic members of the group who ask. You may find that some participants will actually refuse, preferring to reflect on the story in their own way. Some groups, having received the scripts, allocate one participant to read the story again, so that the rest can really take in the content (or it might be just because they enjoyed hearing the story!)

4. Having completed the group exercise, help participants to draw links between the learning or moral of the tale and determine the relevance the story has to your particular issue – whether that be team effectiveness, planning the future, communication. In other words, link back to your purpose for telling the story. Sometimes I take a 'reverse psychology' approach to this, using an almost Socratic questioning style, eg 'What on earth does this story have to do with...?' As they are attempting to convince you, they are also convincing themselves.

Using stories for illustrative purposes

During the course of your training or coaching session, there will be numerous situations where you are trying to explain a complex topic or concept and want to incorporate examples, analogies or stories to help add clarity. There seem to be varying opinions as to the best method for doing this. I tend to use the *premise–story–point* formula. In other words:

● You introduce the concept you are discussing, eg 'There are many different leadership styles.'
● You lead into a relevant story, metaphor or analogy that will help to illustrate the concept, eg 'In fact, I remember the first boss I had who was so unpredictable...'
● You draw the conclusion, eg 'So leaders need to be flexible but consistent...'

This is particularly true if using humour in the story. Humour produces a chemical in the brain that acts like a fixative: it fixes the memory of whatever has gone before. Therefore it makes sense to introduce the premise first, then tell the funny story about the concept and finally return to your point or conclusion. You want participants to remember the concept you are introducing – not just the funny story! However, Shawn Callahan from Australian company Anecdote suggests an alternative approach:

> The conventional presentation format, where we outline our argument first and then follow it up with examples and stories can trigger what psychologists call the 'confirmation bias'. In other words, we are alerted to someone trying to influence us with sophisticated rationale. Instead, why not avoid triggering this bias by starting with examples and stories of what is possible and what we hope to achieve, followed with rational argument.
>
> *www.anecdote.com*

I leave it to you to experiment with these models and see which ones work best for you and the group you are working with.

Using stories for evaluation

Stories can be used to evaluate the effectiveness of a training programme or other human resources project or change management programme. After my last storytelling masterclass workshops, we set up a mastermind group that 'meets' on a tele-conference basis to discuss 'What happened next?' During the call, members can share their experiences from the training, how they have applied the learning, and get group feedback on any problems they have encountered. Another evaluation method, the 'Story dialogue' technique, was developed in Canada by Labonte and Featherstone (1997). It takes the form of a focus group, led by a facilitator and up to six group members, whose aim is to discuss the questions:

1. *What?* Description questions: What were the problems, issues, needs? Who identified them? How did they arise? What did you do? What were the successes or difficulties? How did it turn out?
2. *Why?* Explanation questions: Why do you think it happened? Why did you/they react as you/they did? Why did you do what you did (the strategies or actions)? Why do you think it worked or didn't work?

3. *So what?* Synthesis questions: What have we learned? What remains confusing? How did people or relationships change? What unexpected outcomes occurred?
4. *Now what?* Action questions: What will we do differently next time? What will be our next set of actions? What are the key lessons? What power do we have to do things more effectively in the future and how can we increase this power?

Ending the day with a story

Bet you thought I'd forgotten about this section, didn't you? Using unfinished or nested stories keeps the listener's curiosity going, creates a 'tension gap' and leaves them to ponder (unconsciously) the story during the rest of the session. Finishing the day with 'Before we go, would you like to know what happened to...?' or 'Oh, I forgot – I need to tell you the end to...' lends a nice *gestalt* or wholeness to the day and brings participants back into the Alpha brain levels.

Using different types of story for different effects

The main factors that will determine your choice of story and your way of using it are firstly the type of business issue or problem that you are hoping to address, and secondly the specific purpose that you hope to achieve within that. The issues that you are addressing might include:

- helping the organization clarify the future;
- helping the organization to stand out from the rest;
- making sales presentations more memorable;
- as a means of sharing or clarifying knowledge on a new product or service;
- encouraging a change of culture;
- improving team effectiveness;
- improving leadership effectiveness.

Your purpose within that may be to illustrate a point, to inspire your audience, to motivate them into action, to encourage or accelerate learning, to promote dynamic group discussion, to offer a re-frame or different way of seeing things. Ask yourself: What effects do I want this story to have? What change in thoughts or behaviour would I ultimately like to see? What are the end benefits of using the story? How might telling this story affect the organization? Stephen Denning (2005) advocates the use of a 'note to self' approach to remind yourself of your purpose:

> Put your change idea in writing, preferably in a single sentence. Write the sentence in large letters on a sheet of paper in a prominent place in front of you. Why? In the excitement of telling your story, you will tend to forget the idea that you are trying to communicate. You are likely to lose sight of the purpose for which you're telling the story ... organizational storytelling is a purposeful activity. Keeping the purpose in mind is vital.

I must admit that there have been a few occasions over the years when I have found myself simply enjoying telling a story – and getting pleasure from the audience's reaction, so that I lose track of why I was telling the story in the first place. If you know that you are telling a story mainly for its entertainment or relaxation value, that's fine – the stories in the 'Happy endings' section in Part 2 of this book are intended for just that purpose – but be honest and aware that that's what you're doing. If you try and pass your favourite story off as something deep and meaningful when it actually has no bearing on the topic in hand, you will soon be greeted by 'So what?' reactions from your audience – and lose credibility into the bargain.

Be alert to the fact that there may be secondary and quite legitimate benefits to be gained from using a particular story. I used the story 'Many Moons' by James Thurber (1943) with a group of salespeople, primarily as a tool to illustrate how there can be many different perceptions of what appears to be the same object (in this case the moon), but also found that telling the tale had a surprisingly relaxing effect on the participants and helped to open up their imaginations – which in turn had a very positive and creative impact on their participation during the rest of the workshop.

'Many Moons' is, by business storytelling standards, a long story, taking around 10–15 minutes in the telling. Longer stories, such as 'The town mouse and the country mouse', 'Sunetha's story', 'The elves and the shoemaker' in Part 2 of this book, if told well and with sufficient rapport between you and your listeners, can have a soothing and semi-hypnotic effect; if told badly, without rapport, they just bore the audience. Shorter, snappier stories, like some of the Nasrudin stories or Aesop's fables, tend to increase the pace of learning and the energy levels.

Fairy tales deserve a particular mention here. Sometimes referred to as the purest form of narrative, they allow 'psychological space' for listeners to reflect and add their own interpretations. Bruno Bettelheim (1991) calls them a 'unique art form' and says that their uniqueness lies in their almost one-dimensional narrative style. He says that:

> [T]he fairy tale simplifies all situations. Its figures are clearly drawn; and details, unless very important, are eliminated. All characters are typical rather than unique ... as with all great art, the fairy tale's deepest meaning will be different for each person.

So when we hear stories that follow a fairy-tale template, we are given just enough information to arouse our curiosity and imagination so that we want to identify with the hero or heroine and know more about their struggles within the tale – but not so much that our analytical left brains start to question the authenticity of the story's content. This is a great catalyst, in an organizational setting, for creative discussion.

How to find stories

As well as using the stories in this book, you will probably want to build up your own portfolio for future use. Where do you find good stories? How do you know which ones to choose? Stories are everywhere – but you must have the right filter in your brain to find them. They abound, not just in books on library shelves, but in newspapers and magazines, on television, film and radio. They also hover over bus stops and train stations, and hang in the air around pubs and restaurants. You might find just the right words of wisdom from one of the Greek myths or equally from your next-door neighbour – you never know!

Another excellent source for finding stories is of course the internet. Listed below are some useful websites that will serve as a good starting point for finding additional stories and gaining more information about storytelling in organizations:

www.astoriedcareer.com

www.nationalstorytelling.net

www.sfs.org.uk

www.storycorps.com

www.success-stories.co.uk

www.storynet.org

www.storytellingcenter.net

For those who prefer the original book format for story gathering, there is a huge number of resources available, including my own previous books in the *Tales* series, all of which are listed in the 'References and further reading' section at the back of this book.

You will also find that you become a good 'story listener' within your own organization. With a little encouragement, people are happy to tell you about their own experiences at work or at home; your job is to assess the suitability of these as potential learning material. Stories told within the organization tend to fall into these main categories:

1. *Didn't we do well!*
    What we're most proud of; an achievement; some formal recognition.

2. *Cautionary tales*
    We learnt from our mistakes; things could have gone wrong if we hadn't...; we found a solution because of this problem.

3. *Tales of courage*
    We survived against all the odds; we pulled out all the stops.

4. *Hero/heroine stories*
    The person who goes beyond the call of duty; sometimes a 'tribal elder' or founder of the organization who has many years of experience.

5. *Letting-off-steam stories*
    Told for stress relief and relaxation; survival stories; very often told in emergency-services organizations.

Adapted from Neuhauser, 1993

When considering the suitability of any internal stories to include in your training workshops or meetings, or for other learning purposes, the following questions might be helpful:

- Is the person willing to share their story?
- Should the tale be told anonymously or is the contributor willing to put their name to it?
- Why does their story resonate with me?
- Would it resonate with a learning group in the same way?
- Are the language, culture, values and message conveyed appropriate to this particular learning group?
- Might the story cause offence to anyone?
- What message would I like this story to convey?
- Is it an enlightening message – or a cautionary tale?
- How should I use the story – written or verbal, word for word or précised?
- Who should tell the story? Is the person who contributed it a good storyteller?
- Should the story be edited in any way?
- When should I use the story – to illustrate a particular point during training, for reflection prior to or after the training?

Telling the tale – incorporating the storyteller's skills

> The trouble with telling a good story is that it invariably reminds the other fellow of a dull one.
>
> *Sid Caesar*

Introductions and transitions

The transition into telling a story in a business setting is one of the key deciders as to whether it will be successful or not. I find that the best way is to aim for a seamless link from your ordinary speaking voice into telling the tale, almost so that the audience doesn't realize that they are being told a story. Professional storyteller Jack Maguire (1998) compares the aim of good storytelling to gently planting a 'timed-release explosive charge' within the listener's mind. He says:

It may not go off at the time of implant ... the dynamic usually occurs when a teller communicates a good story of any kind in an essentially 'ordinary' voice. The tale sneaks into the listener's mind, rather than making a dramatic entrance.

The worst thing you can do is to have a huge hiatus, followed by the use of a highly pitched, kindergarten-type voice. This can make your participants very nervous – and embarrassed for you; they start to wonder at what point you might break into a song and dance. Please remember that, in business storytelling, you are an adult talking to other adults, and you are using a story for a specific business-related reason. This doesn't mean that you have to tell the story stony faced, but there is no need for huge dramatization unless you feel it appropriate. Just use your normal conversational voice, at least until you are sure your audience is hooked on the story and they go into an Alpha state, at which point you can experiment with slowing down the pace of your voice to help maintain that state. You might find the following transitional links useful:

- That reminds me of a time when...
- Did you hear about...
- An example of that would be...
- Let me show you what I mean...
- I heard the other day that...

Or if you particularly want to stimulate curiosity (as mentioned in Chapter 1), use these types of openings:

- Don't tell anyone else, but...
- I don't know if you know this, but...
- Have you heard?...
- You'll never guess what happened when...
- I must tell you...

If you're overtly making a feature of using a story, you can experiment with the traditional 'Once upon a time', or 'Are you sitting comfortably?' but be careful – these openers carry with them an element of risk, and you want to ensure that your listeners are thinking in a child-*like* not child*ish* mind set. If they have any sense of being coerced into the latter, they will undoubtedly resist you, the brains will go shooting back into the Beta levels and you will undo any good that you might have done.

Empathy

The original storytellers had a natural rapport with their audiences; we need to make sure that, whenever possible, we know the audience, what they will find useful and what not, what sort of language is appropriate, etc. It's also advisable – certainly initially – to tell stories that meet your audience in their world rather than attempting to drag them into yours. Your aim is for engagement and flow rather than resistance. This is why, particularly during any introduction to a talk or training session, I try to avoid 'me' stories, focusing instead on 'them'. Customize your story wherever you can, if possible incorporating names, symbols, or in-jokes from the audience. Maintaining regular eye contact with all your participants while you are telling your story also helps to demonstrate empathy and builds good communication; it gives you the opportunity to judge how they are responding to you and also helps to involve the listener so that they feel they are part of the story.

Participation

Another of the side effects of good storytelling is that it acts as a trigger in the minds of those who hear it. You may well find that your learners, while hearing your story, want to contribute their own experiences, possibly to put themselves in the position of hero or possibly to align themselves to you. Whatever the reason, if you feel it to be relevant and appropriate to your topic, their participation should be encouraged – but also managed carefully, so that the purpose of the storytelling isn't hijacked.

Humour

This is the bedrock of good storytelling – although any attempts at incorporating humour must be appropriate to the context and enjoyed equally between you and your audience. If you are laughing and your audience isn't, the humour is not appropriate. Be careful to make it obvious what is supposed to be amusing and what isn't. You do this mainly through your use of voice and non-verbal communication. Be sure not to give mixed signals, so that your audience doesn't know whether they should be laughing or not. Some group members a while ago told me that I had a natural comedic presence in my presentation style which was a huge compliment – but not if I'm attempting to tell a sad or serious tale! If you don't feel comfortable using humour, avoid it; don't attempt to tell jokes and certainly don't pause for laughter – it may never come!

Imagery

As previously mentioned, the use of vivid and memorable imagery was one of the fundamentals of the original storytellers. The purpose of imagery is to invoke sensory stimulus: the listener will be drawn into the story by being able to visualize the narrative in their own way. Imagery can also include symbolic representation and metaphor, which add colour, interest and often humour to a story – particularly if they're in the bizarre category like some of the lines from the TV series, *Blackadder*, whose writers, Richard Curtis and Ben Elton, turned the process into a sophisticated art form. These are two examples of Blackadder talking to his long-suffering manservant, Baldrick:

> You wouldn't recognize a subtle plan if it painted itself purple and danced naked on a harpsichord singing 'Subtle plans are here again.'

> This is a crisis; a large crisis. In fact, if you've got a moment, it's a 12-storey crisis with a magnificent entrance hall, carpeting throughout, 24-hour porterage and an enormous sign on the roof, saying 'This Is a Large Crisis'.

Repetition

We expect to find repetition in a good story. Think back to your days of listening to 'Little Red Riding Hood' and you'll know what I mean. Repetition encourages involvement in the tale. In business storytelling, careful use of repetition emphasizes certain elements of the narrative and encourages belief in the listener. It also lodges in the memory banks and helps the imagination to activate. For example, the sentence 'The company grew' doesn't really do much to stir the blood. But the sentence 'The company grew ... and grew ... and grew ... and grew' paints a completely different and more colourful picture, and acts as an intensifier to the emotional content.

Exaggeration

Another ploy for intensifying content is exaggeration. We all know the fisherman's story of 'It was *this big*!' Most professional storytellers exaggerate, but if you're using this technique for organizational purposes, you need to make clear to the audience that whatever you're saying is an exaggeration and not necessarily true. For example, I wouldn't recommend exaggerating your company's financial status – well, not to your bank manager anyway. If your exaggerated comment is accompanied with a humorous or wry expression, the audience will usually get the point. In business storytelling I would advise limiting your exaggeration to the content of your story rather than your delivery – I mentioned before the dangers of donning a jester's outfit. It is worth remembering that we have to balance our urge for creativity with the need for credibility.

Another novel verbal technique for intensification is in using negative words to describe positive verbs. For example: 'She was disgustingly healthy,' 'He came up with an insanely simple idea,' 'She had a sickeningly good voice.' This is a powerful technique in that it borrows the strength and intensity of the negative emotion and combines it unexpectedly with positive words, thus causing temporary confusion and destabilization in the brain which, as we discussed in Chapter 1, can invigorate the learning and memory processes.

Bring the story alive through use of voice

Be aware of the tone, pitch, pace, volume and colour in your own voice and match these where you can to those of your audience. This is another way of gaining rapport with them. Modulating the tones and pace of your voice will create interest and enthusiasm and establish the mood you are trying to create – but don't over-dramatize. For example, it would be perfectly acceptable to make the word '*exciting*!' sound exciting, but I wouldn't necessarily suggest that at the same time you leap up and down on a table waving your arms in the air ... apart from anything else, you might hurt yourself!

Include dialogue to bring characters to life and maintain interest in the story, but here again don't overdo your range of voices. Very slight changes in your voice are sufficient to make the point that this is someone else speaking. Use pausing for dramatic effect, but don't make the pauses so long and frequent that your audience becomes irritated or anxious on your behalf that you've forgotten the words. Pauses can be added in many places to add impact – for example:

- Pause before a punchline or an important point in the story.
- Pause after a punchline or an important point in the story to let it sink in.
- Combine pauses with dramatic action, such as uncovering a prop or pointing to something important.
- Pause between repetitions to heighten impact, eg 'She grew ... and grew.'
- Use non-verbal signals to emphasize the pause, eg freezing the body, perhaps with an expectant expression on your face.
- Pause as you come to the end of the story.

Whenever you use a pause, do ensure that, from your audience's point of view, it is worth the wait; if the outcome doesn't match the drama that you have attempted to create, you will cause disappointment as well as losing rapport.

You can also change the mood and pace of your story by changing the pace of your voice. Make sure that you speak slowly and clearly enough for your words to be heard, but not so slowly that your audience becomes bored. If you are describing something that happened very s–l–o–w–l–y or you are reaching the end of the story, you can of course use your voice to reinforce the action of the narrative or stress the importance of the end line. Be careful, though, not to drop the volume or tone of your voice at the end or climax of the piece so that your audience is left wondering and asking each other, 'What did she say?' This can destroy the whole atmosphere and leave people feeling annoyed that they have sat expectantly for 10 minutes only to have missed the whole point of the story. If you'd like to hear some audio examples of my own storytelling, visit the Kogan Page website at: www.koganpage.com.

Non-verbal communication

An old adage in storytelling is 'Show, don't tell.' In other words, your body and facial expression should always be congruent with the tale you are telling, unless you are very obviously being sarcastic or ironic. If it's a happy story, look happy; if it's sad, look sad; if it's dramatic, look dramatic (within reason). Above all, appear confident – if you look unsure, your audience will pick this up and react to your embarrassment.

Use gestures and posture to add further impact to the key elements of your story. For example, when I come to the section of 'The goose that laid the golden eggs' in which 'the farmer's wife looked at the egg, looked at the goose and looked at the farmer', I look to various parts of the room to reinforce each part of the sentence. When Carly Read told her story about Ann (see 'Carly's story' in Part 2), the indolent worker who had 'her evening newspaper semi-hidden in her desk drawer, which she would deftly elbow shut whenever I passed by her office', she quite naturally imitated the action by using her elbows to close the mock drawers that she was describing – a gesture that stuck in my mind for some time after the telling. Jack Maguire (1998) gives good advice on the use of body language in storytelling:

> Don't strain yourself to create physical images or moves that don't suggest themselves naturally ... if you're not very expressive with your face or body in everyday life, then you're very likely to feel and look weird morphing into a mime to deliver a story.

Above all, your storytelling should look and sound like you, not a copy of someone else. You want to adopt a style that you feel comfortable with and that you and your audience can trust and enjoy. Remember, you are simply a conduit for the story – your telling should feel like a seamless enhancement of the content, not a detraction from it. Think of you and the story you are telling as being one and the same entity – impossible to tell where one begins and the other ends.

Don't think you have to be perfect

I still find that many trainers and coaches love the idea of incorporating storytelling into their portfolio of skills, but admit to feeling nervous of taking the first metaphorical leap. If you would like further guidance on business storytelling, you can visit my website at www.success-stories.co.uk, where there are lots of practical tips and techniques, or you might like to join me on a storytelling workshop that we run several times a year – details in 'Further information' towards the end of this book.

But the most important thing is not to think that your storytelling delivery has to be perfect – in fact, it's sometimes better if it isn't. Some time ago I attended a workshop where the facilitator began the day by suggesting that we all draw metaphor pictures to depict our preferred method of learning, 'For example,' she said, holding up her own Dalí-esque masterpiece, 'here is mine.' Well, I don't know about you, but I couldn't draw my way out of a tight spot, and I was horrified at the prospect of the humiliation that was to come. I nearly left the workshop on the spot, saying, 'Sorry – wrong course.' It wasn't the idea in principle – which was good – it was her showing her own example, with the distinct implication, 'You should do something like this.' The instruction was, to my mind, too limiting and rather contradicted the very nature of metaphor.

So, in the same way, practise your story, but not to the extent that you sound sterile and over-scripted. Expect that there may be some stumbling and stuttering and you might even get the words wrong. This only goes to make you and the story more believable. The same applies to any colleagues that may be attempting to tell stories for the first time – I'm very often asked the question, 'Is that right?' to which of course the answer is 'Yes, your story is your story – how could it be wrong?'

To sum up...

- Business storytelling is a different genre to children's storytelling.
- Storytelling should be introduced subtly and labelled carefully – better in some cases to call it 'business narrative'.
- Stories can be used as part of an induction programme to bring the organization to life.
- You can use stories before a training or coaching session, to encourage learners to think and reflect.
- Unfinished or 'nested' stories can be used during training sessions to prolong learning and stimulate curiosity.
- Stories can be used to stimulate creative discussion.
- Stories can be used to illustrate a complex topic.
- Stories can be used as part of your evaluation process – either individually or in focus groups.
- Different types of story produce different effects – your choice will depend on your desired outcome.
- Where to find good stories – both inside and outside your organization.
- Practise incorporating the storyteller's skills – including empathy, participation, humour, imagery, repetition and exaggeration.

- Use your voice – tone, pitch, pace, volume, pausing – to bring the story to life.
- Use non-verbal communication to enhance your story – not to detract from it.

Part 2

And then one day ...

ENLIGHTENING TALES

This first collection of tales is intended to help understanding, to increase one's knowledge or wisdom and to dispel ignorance. They can shine a light on a difficult or complex topic. They provide food for thought and encourage reflective thinking. The collection consists of twenty stories, drawn from various sources ranging from the teachings of Buddha and the Sufis to Bob Geldof and Yoko Ono.

The stories can be used to shed light on such topics as: self-belief, dealing with conflict, problem solving, emotional intelligence, leadership and influence.

▌ Nasrudin and the tigers

The mullah Nasrudin (called variously 'Nasruddin' or 'Nasreddin'), a legendary Sufi character of the 13th century, is always written about in such a way that we are never sure whether he is extremely wise or extremely foolish. And I'm not the one to elucidate here either – I leave you to make up your own mind!

A neighbour came across the mullah Nasrudin, walking round his house, scattering breadcrumbs as he went. After watching him for a while, he said, 'Nasrudin, why are you throwing breadcrumbs all around your house?'

Nasrudin, without stopping his work, said, 'I'm keeping the tigers away.'

After a moment or two of reflection, his neighbour said, 'But Nasrudin, there are no tigers in this part of the country.'

'I know,' grinned Nasrudin triumphantly. 'It works well, doesn't it!

Reference: A much-told Nasrudin story. More stories are available from the author Idries Shah at: www.idriesshah.com.

Reflection

Are we looking for a solution for a problem that doesn't exist? Or are we wise to use preventative measures?

This story could be used for:

Learning and development.

Problem solving.

Project management.

Talking points

Do you think Nasrudin's actions were wise or foolish?

In your organization, how do you gather genuine evidence as to whether something works?

Are resources wasted on finding solutions for problems that don't exist?

2 In the hands of destiny

Zen stories offered a very special form of teaching – their purpose was to encourage self-discovery through meditation and contemplation.

A great Japanese warrior named Nobunaga decided to attack the enemy, although he had only one-tenth the number of men the opposition commanded. He was confident that he would win, but his soldiers were in doubt. On the way, he stopped at a Shinto shrine and told his men: 'After I visit the shrine I will toss a coin. If it is heads, we will win; if it is tails, we will lose. Destiny holds us in her hand.'

Nobunaga entered the shrine and offered a silent prayer. He came out and tossed a coin. It came up heads. His soldiers were then so eager to fight that they won their battle easily.

'No one can change the hand of destiny,' his attendant said after the battle.

'Indeed not,' said Nobunaga, showing a coin that was double-sided, with heads facing either way.

Reference: Reps, P (2000) *Zen Flesh, Zen Bones*, Penguin, London.

Reflection

As Zen stories were originally intended to encourage self-discovery, there is usually neither a moral nor a definitive right answer given. However, the story prompts lively discussion for leaders and teams on beliefs, values and notions of integrity and self-belief.

This story could be used for:

Leadership.

Teamwork.

Positive thinking.

Self-belief.

Integrity.

Talking points

Was Nobunaga right in his handling of the situation?

Was he deceiving his men or helping them?

Can you imagine the story if the coin had come up tails?

What alternative approach could Nobunaga have taken?

How might this style of leadership be perceived in a modern business setting?

3 Worlds apart

Colin Turnbull, the famous anthropologist and explorer, was best known for his work with the Mbuti tribe of equatorial Africa, the only tribe who can truly be called pygmies, being under 150 cm in height. The pygmies live in the dense rainforests of central Africa. Theirs is essentially a 'vertical world', where horizons and horizontal landscapes are unknown. The pygmies, like all of us, have adapted and evolved over the centuries to accommodate their world, so much so that if they are ever forced to leave it, for the likes of, say, the flat plains of Africa, they become very anxious, even nauseous, and find it hard to make sense of their surroundings.

Turnbull writes of his Mbuti friend, Kenge, and his experience of the African savannah. Kenge found it hard to understand the appearance of snow on the tops of some of the mountains, and remained unconvinced by Turnbull's explanation of it being water in a different format. Instead, he stuck to his own account of it being 'some kind of white rock'.

When he saw buffalo grazing in the distance some miles away, he turned to Turnbull and said, 'What sort of insects are those?' When Turnbull told his friend that they were buffalo, Kenge roared with laughter, 'Don't tell lies!' he exclaimed. 'How can those tiny things be buffalo?' It was futile to attempt any other explanation about distance or perspective. As they drove nearer and nearer, however, and the 'miniature' buffalo grew rapidly larger, Turnbull was curious as to what was going through his friend's mind. How did he explain this apparent transformation to himself – did he think that the 'insects' were now turning into buffalo, or did he think that the miniature buffalo were just growing bigger and bigger by the minute? But Kenge remained silent, preferring not to share his thoughts. His only parting comment, as they got out of the car, was to shrug and say, 'Not real buffalo,' as though no one could take him for a fool.

Reference: An extract from Turnbull, C (1961) *Forest People*, Jonathan Cape, London.

Reflection

Although we might smile at the apparent limitations of Kenge's thinking, we might just as easily be accused of similar blinkered vision when taken out of our own comfort zone or exposed to new people or situations.

This story could be used for:

Equality and diversity.

Emotional intelligence (understanding self and others).

Perceptions.

Induction into a new area or job.

Talking points

What do you think is the message of the story?

Can you relate Kenge's experience to your own or that of others?

Do you think of Kenge as an intelligent man?

Should Turnbull have handled the situation differently?

Is it right to criticize or disbelieve the surroundings just because they do not relate to our own experience?

4 The chess set

I heard this story on the news some weeks ago, and, like all good stories, it started me thinking...

Yoko Ono, sometimes dubbed 'the woman who broke up the Beatles', was a talented and well-respected artist long before her association with John Lennon. In 1966, she created a giant chess set – a stunning chessboard and pieces, some 16 ft square.

At first glance, the sculpture looks like a conventional (if very large) chessboard – knights, pawns, bishops, all are there. But there is actually nothing conventional about it. All the chess pieces are white. And all the pieces sit on a board made up only of white squares. As you look at it, you wonder how a game of chess might be played. Yoko Ono intended it to be a thought-provoking piece of art with a political message. She named it 'Play It by Trust'.

Source: Television article; entry in www.wikipedia.co.uk.

Reflection

'Play It by Trust' is currently displayed at the LongHouse Gallery, East Hampton near New York. Its message could either be that for any game to be possible, one would have to rely on one's opponent's honesty (and your own) – hence the title of the piece – or to highlight the futility of conflict, as both sides are essentially the same.

This story could be used for:

Perceptions.

Communication.

Dealing with conflict.

Emotional intelligence (understanding self and others).

Talking points

What was the message that Yoko Ono was trying to convey with this piece?

What is the significance of the title: 'Play It by Trust'?

How might a game of chess be played on this board?

What does the story tell you about conflict, confrontation, competition?

5 Beating the drum

This is a traditional Sufi tale that can be used to illustrate the need to see things from a different point of view and also to highlight the power of the unexpected or 're-frame'.

Once there was a small boy whose grandma had given him a drum for his birthday. He loved the drum very much, and played with it all day long – bang, bang, bang – much to the annoyance of his parents and neighbours. The parents begged the young boy to stop, but he ignored them and just carried on – bang, bang, bang – all the day. The parents, in desperation, sought the help of a wise and respected doctor.

'Please get our child to stop banging the drum!' they cried. The doctor tried explaining to the child how the constant noise was damaging his eardrums. But the advice was too advanced for the child, who didn't know what an eardrum was, so he went on playing.

The parents called in a wise and respected teacher. 'Please get our child to stop banging the drum!' they cried. The teacher tried giving the boy a book of instructions, saying that if he read the book his drum playing would improve. But the child found the instruction book too long and boring and so he abandoned it and went on playing.

The parents sought the help of a psychiatrist. 'Please get our child to stop banging the drum!' they cried. The psychiatrist gave the boy some meditation exercises and some lessons in anger management, but all that happened was that the boy slowed down his playing – for a short while – and then, refreshed, would start playing again all the more vigorously.

Then a Sufi, a wise man, who happened to be passing, heard the tale of the little boy and the drum. He listened to the child for a short while and then handed the boy a hammer and chisel, saying, 'I wonder if you can find out what's inside this drum?'

Reference: Retold traditional Sufi tale.

Reflection

People don't change their behaviour just because you want them to. We all choose to make changes, and there has to be a personal motivation that prompts the person to change their behaviour – either the potential pleasure to be gained or the potential pain to be avoided.

This story could be used for:

Dealing with change.

Creativity.

Problem solving.

Learning and development.

Talking points

Why did the Sufi succeed when others failed?

Can you relate this story to any of your own experiences in trying to persuade someone to change?

What might have been an alternative (non-violent!) end to the story?

6 The rich and the poor

A good tale for helping to put things into perspective and also for showing that learning doesn't always take place in the conventional ways that we think it should. (See Chapter 1 for more on informal learning.)

One day, the father of a wealthy family took his son on a trip far out into a remote part of the country, with the aim of showing his privileged son how poor people lived. He left his son at the house of a poor farmer he knew, where he had arranged for him to spend two days and two nights. When he went to pick him up, the father asked his son, 'How was your stay?'

The boy said, 'It was great, Dad.'

'And did you learn about how poor people live?' asked the father.

'Oh yes, Dad,' replied the boy.

'What in particular did you learn, Son?'

The son answered, 'Well, I learnt that we have one dog and they have four. We have a pool just in the middle of our garden and they have a creek that has no end. We have plastic lanterns in our garden, but from their garden they can see thousands of stars at night. We have a small piece of land where our house was built and they have fields as far as you can see. We have servants who serve us, but they spend all their time serving others and helping their community and it makes them happy. We buy our food from the supermarket, but they grow all theirs. We have walls and security around our property to protect us, but they have friends and neighbours who protect them.'

The boy's father was speechless. Then his son added, 'I think I learnt how poor we really are.'

Reference: Adapted from a story on www.inspirationalstories.com.

Reflection

This story teaches us that everything is relative: what is wealth to one person may constitute poverty to another (and vice versa). It also cautions us to be aware that others may absorb different points of learning from the ones that you intended.

This story could be used for:

Empowerment/engagement.

Knowledge sharing.

Learning and development.

Positive thinking.

Perceptions.

Talking points

Was this an effective way of learning?

What was the expected outcome?

Was this still a 'good' lesson?

Can you imagine the story from the poor farmer's point of view?

Who learnt the most?

7 Lauren Luke: changing the face of beauty

The name may not be immediately recognizable to some, but Lauren Luke is 'the one off the internet' who started what is now a multi-million-pound business from her pink bedroom in South Shields in the north of England.

Something of a modern business success story, Lauren Luke was working as a taxi dispatcher when she had the idea to buy wholesale make-up to sell on Ebay, and demonstrate to other women how to use it, applying it on herself and then taking a photo to post on the internet. Soon she had so many replies that she found it easier to upload demonstration videos that would serve as tutorials for those who wanted to copy her style. She never does 'make-overs' for other people, saying, 'I think it's better for people to be able to do it for themselves.'

Never having had a make-up lesson in her life, Lauren simply invents her own rules; she also makes mistakes – all in real time. Her videos are not professionally shot; there is no airbrushing, no actors are employed, and the videos are never edited – 'I didn't know how,' she says. And yet her fans (of whom there are now some 17 million worldwide) lap up her down-to-earth, friendly and personable approach. She speaks directly to the camera, sometimes mispronouncing the brand names, and sometimes being openly critical of some of the products she has discovered. 'You don't have to fart about with that,' she says.

Lauren admits to having had a lack of confidence that dates back to her schooldays, where she was bullied and taunted for being 'the plain Jane' of the classroom, and where it was assumed by her teachers that she would 'amount to nothing'. She took to using make-up as a form of refuge against her aggressors, hoping that it would make her more likeable. 'It worked with the boys,' she smiles.

Her down-to-earth and natural style is the antithesis to the false, intimidating, airbrushed face of the beauty industry. 'I think people have had enough,' she says. 'They want people to be shown as they really are. I think I've come along at a good time for that.'

Source: Television article; articles in www.bylaurenluke.com and www.wikipedia.co.uk

Reflection

One could say that this is a classic case of 'She didn't know what she didn't know.' Sometimes it pays not to know the 'correct' procedure.

This story could be used for:

Branding/marketing.

Emotional intelligence (understanding self and others).

Empowerment/engagement.

Positive thinking.

Self-belief.

Talking points

What are your feelings about Lauren's style of doing business?

She prefers to teach people how to apply make-up rather than do it for them. Is this a good strategy?

Do you agree with her statement that 'people have had enough'?

Was Lauren's lack of training as a make-up artist a help or a hindrance?

What does this tell us about the relevance of training and development in an organizational context?

8 The doctor's remedy

I'm indebted to my friend and colleague Lenn Millbower for this illustrative and amusing story. He told me: 'A patient goes to the doctor to get advice. Below is a transcript of what transpired in the doctor's office...'

Monday

'Doc, I'm having trouble sleeping,' said the patient. 'It's not that something's bothering me. Or at least, anything I can put a finger on. I simply can't sleep. Counting sheep, drinking wine, taking a hot bath, taking a cold shower: none of it worked.'

'I see,' said the doctor. 'Take two of these pills before you go to sleep and call me on Wednesday.'

Wednesday

'Doc, I still can't sleep,' said the patient. 'I'm exhausted. I need relief.'

'I see,' said the doctor. 'Let's double the dosage. Take two of these pills before you go to sleep and call me on Friday.'

Friday

'Doc, it's just not working,' said the patient. 'Can we increase the dose again?'

'That could be dangerous,' said the doctor. 'But wait. I've got a better idea. Try this.'

'Doc, what am I supposed to do with this machine?' asked the patient.

'Take it home, plug it in, turn it on, and aim it at the wall,' said the doctor. 'You should be asleep in minutes.'

'I don't understand. What is it?'

'My office delivers in-service training for the staff. It's a projector loaded with our 45-minute slide presentation. If that doesn't put you to sleep, nothing will.'

Source: Lenn Millbower. www.offbeattraining.com

Reflection

When PowerPoint was originally designed it was intended as a creative tool to enhance a presentation. But too many presenters see it as a replacement for them, and this is when it starts to lose its impact. Some of the best presentations I have seen contained no slides at all.

This story could be used for:

Presentation skills.

Communication.

Learning and development.

Talking points

Can you relate to the implicit warning in this story?

Have you been guilty yourself of over-reliance on slides and visuals?

How could you improve a presentation to make it more accessible?

How might you coach others in better presentation skills without reliance on visuals?

9 The Wonderful Wizard of Oz

Perhaps one of the best stories ever written, this classic by L Frank Baum continues to delight audiences old and young, and can be enjoyed on many different levels.

After the Wizard has been revealed as not really a Wizard at all, but a bit of a 'humbug' as Dorothy calls him, the three friends lament the fact that they may never achieve what they set out for – brains, courage and love...

'I think you are a very bad man,' said Dorothy.

'Oh no, my dear; I'm really a very good man; but I'm a very bad Wizard, I must admit.'

'Can't you give me brains?' asked the Scarecrow.

'You don't need them. You are learning something every day. A baby has brains, but it doesn't know much. Experience is the only thing that brings knowledge, and the longer you are on earth the more experience you are sure to get.'

'But what about my courage?' asked the Lion, anxiously.

'You have plenty of courage, I am sure,' answered Oz. 'All you need is confidence in yourself. There is no living thing that is not afraid when it faces danger, and that kind of courage you have in plenty.'

'How about my heart?' asked the Tin Woodman.

'Why, as for that,' answered Oz, 'I think you are wrong to want a heart. It makes most people unhappy. If you only knew it, you are in luck not to have a heart.'

'That must be a matter of opinion,' said the Tin Man. 'For my part, I will bear all the unhappiness without a murmur, if you will give me the heart.'

'Very well,' answered Oz meekly. 'Come to me tomorrow and you shall have a heart.'

He sighed and said to himself, 'I have played the Wizard for so many years that I may as well continue the part a little longer.'

Reference: An adapted extract from *The Wonderful Wizard of Oz*, written by L Frank Baum, originally published by the George M Hill Company in 1900.

Reflection

Many scholars say that *The Wonderful Wizard of Oz* is an allegory or metaphor for the political, economic and social events of America of the 1890s, with Dorothy portraying Everyman, the cyclone representing political unrest, and the Munchkins representing the little people or ordinary citizens. Whatever your preferred theory, the story is still a powerful tool for discussion.

This story could be used for:

Realistic goal setting.

Integrity/humility.

Perceptions.

Self-belief.

Talking points

Do you agree with the Wizard's remarks about brains and courage?

Is it better to be heartless as the Wizard suggests?

Can you relate to any (or all) of the three?

Was the Wizard 'a very bad man' to have pretended to the inhabitants of Oz for all those years?

10 The real king

Indian poet and author Mahesh Das grew up poor but educated. As an adult he became renowned for his wit and wisdom, and was invited to join the court of the Emperor Akbar, who gave him a new name, Birbal ('Bir' meaning 'brain' and 'bal' meaning 'strong'). Not surprisingly, a number of tales have sprung up over the years, illustrating Birbal's wisdom.

The King of Iran had heard that Birbal was one of the wisest men in the East and, eager to meet him, sent him an invitation to visit his country. In due course, Birbal arrived in Iran. When he entered the palace he was flabbergasted to find not one but six kings seated there. All looked alike. All were dressed in kingly robes. Who was the real king? The very next moment he got his answer. Confidently, Birbal approached the king and bowed to him.

'But how did you identify me?' the king asked, puzzled.

Birbal smiled and explained: 'The false kings were all looking at you, while you yourself looked straight ahead. Even in regal robes, the common people will always look to their king for support.'

Overjoyed, the king embraced Birbal and showered him with gifts.

Reference: A retold traditional story. More Indian folk tales can be found at www.dimdima.com.

Reflection

It is a useful strategy, in a training session or meeting, if you want to know the person in the group with the most influence, to start the workshop with an innocuous question such as 'Shall we open the windows?' If you watch carefully, the chances are that all eyes in the group will go to the 'key influencer' or decision maker in the group.

This story could be used for:

Communication.

Creativity.

Emotional intelligence (understanding self and others).

Influence.

Leadership.

Teamwork.

Talking points

Do you agree with Birbal's strategy?

Should others 'look to their king for support'?

Who are the key influencers inside and outside your organization? How do you know?

What is your influencing style?

Could you employ a similar technique to Birbal's?

11 The town mouse and the country mouse

A slightly modernized version of the old Aesop classic – but still with a timeless message.

Once there were two little mice – one lived in style and splendour in a big house in the town and the other lived under a hedge at the edge of a big field in the country. One day Joshua, the country mouse, thought to himself, 'I must invite my cousin Angus to come for a short holiday. It's a lovely time of the year here in the country; the hedges and trees are all in full bloom and there is plenty to eat. I'm sure he'd love it.'

So sure enough, a few days later, Angus arrived from his home in the town, carrying his Louis Vuitton bag under his arm and sporting a fine waistcoat and trousers. But when he looked around Joshua's little home, he wrinkled his nose in disapproval.

'Forgive me, cousin,' he said, lifting his tail carefully so that it wouldn't trail in the mud, 'but I had no idea you lived in such poverty. You must come back with me to the city, and experience *real* living.'

And so the next day, after Angus had spent a miserable night avoiding raindrops from the leaves of the hedge and attempting to hide his distaste at the nuts and berries that he was offered for his supper, the two set off together to Angus's home in the town.

'Now this is what a home should be!' he exclaimed proudly, as he ushered Joshua through the hole in the skirting board and into the larder where the cook kept all the food. Joshua gasped when he saw the huge spread laid out before him. But it was not the sort of food that he was used to – there was rich cheese, meat, cake and some delicious-smelling chocolate – it was difficult to know where to start. But no sooner had they begun to tuck in than Angus shouted, '*Cat!*' and bolted towards the skirting board again, dragging his petrified cousin behind him.

Much to Joshua's dismay, this incident set the scene for the rest of the day. Every time the two little mice started their supper, the cat would appear menacingly at the larder door and they would need to dash back to safety. Soon Joshua was exhausted; his nerves were shattered, he was starting to get indigestion with the constant interruptions to their meal – even the chocolate didn't taste so good.

At the end of the day, having survived the latest onslaught from the cat, the country mouse said, 'Thank you indeed, cousin, for your kind hospitality, but I couldn't live like this. My nerves are in shreds. I must get back to the peace and quiet of the country. I don't think I can stand much more of this ... uuh ... excitement.'

And with that, he picked up his belongings, which he kept in a tiny scrap of cloth, and headed back to his own little home under the hedge. His cousin Angus was left pondering and stroking his whiskers thoughtfully.

'There's no accounting for taste,' he said.

Reference: Retold Aesop fable. The original featured in Lord, J V and Michie, J (1989) *Aesop's Fables*, Jonathan Cape, London.

Reflection

I suppose the moral 'Each to his own' is the best fit for the tale. Although we talk glibly about 'being in someone else's shoes' we rarely, if ever, manage to do it.

This story could be used for:

Dealing with change.

Emotional intelligence (understanding self and others).

Perceptions.

Realistic goal setting.

Talking points

What does the story tell you about people's perceptions?

Which was the 'best' environment to live in?

To what degree do we really try to understand another person's 'map' of the world?

In a business context, what are the consequences of forcing a change of environment on someone?

12 Learning to learn

This is a traditional Chinese tale that illustrates the effort and consistency required in learning.

During the Dong Jin dynasty, the famous poet Tao Yuanming was a noble and knowledgeable scholar. A young man said to him, 'I admire you because you are so knowledgeable. Would you tell me the best way to learn?'

Tao Yuanming said, 'There is no best way. If you work hard, you will make progress. And if you slack off, you will lag behind.' He took the young man by the hand and guided him to a field. He pointed at a small sprout and said, 'Look carefully. Can you see it growing?' The young man stared at it for a long time and said, 'I did not see it grow.' Tao Yuanming asked, 'Really? Then how could a little sprout become so tall later on?' He continued, 'In fact, it is growing every moment. However, we cannot see it with our eyes. It is the same principle for learning. Our knowledge accumulates little by little. Sometimes we don't even know it. But if you consistently do it, you will make great progress.'

Tao Yuanming then pointed to a knife-sharpening stone next to the stream and asked the young man, 'Why is the concave side of the stone worn down like a saddle?' The young man answered, 'It is because people use it to sharpen knives day after day.' Tao Yuanming then asked, 'Then on exactly which day did it take this shape?' The young man shook his head. Tao Yuanming said, 'It is because farmers have used it day after day. Learning is the same. If you don't do it consistently, you will go backwards.'

The young man finally understood him. He thanked Tao Yuanming. Tao wrote the following for him: 'Learning diligently is like a sprout in the spring. It grows although we can't see its daily growth. Slacking off is like not using a knife-sharpening stone. You will lose if you can't study consistently.'

Reference: An extract from www.talesofwisdom.com.

Reflection

For learning to be effective it needs a consistent and diligent approach. Some people begin a learning programme full of enthusiasm and energy, but they almost apply too much energy to it and very quickly burn out. Better to take a steady and regular approach to learning.

This story could be used for:

Induction into a new area or job.

Learning and development.

Motivation and reward.

Talent management.

Talking points

How does this story fit with the learning culture in your organization?

Are others encouraged to learn gradually and consistently?

What might the dangers be of learning too quickly?

How is consistency in learning rewarded in your organization?

13 Sunetha's story

Sunetha is now a very successful scientist working for a medical research company. She was born in South Africa to Indian parents. During one of our coaching sessions she talked about her first experience of work at a time when the country was going through some radical reform.

I remember applying for jobs as an analytical scientist in South Africa. I applied for a particular job where, as part of the application, I had to write an essay about myself – what I thought of myself, what I thought of other people and how I viewed the world. In the final section I took a bold move and wrote about how I looked forward to the day when racial barriers were broken down. After I had sent in the application I started wondering whether I had done the right thing – this company employed only white people. I thought, 'Sunetha, you've really shot yourself in the foot!' Anyway, much to my surprise, I got the job.

I'll never forget my first few days there. *Every single person was white.* I was the only Indian person there. Even the cleaners were white, and for me that was shocking because the cleaners in South Africa were always black. It was scary initially – it kept going through my mind: 'How am I going to fit in here? How are people going to treat me?' There were a lot of people who couldn't speak English; they just spoke Afrikaans so I had to speak in their language, which made it doubly difficult as my Afrikaans is not that great. Some of them wouldn't try to speak English because they were frightened of looking inferior if they mispronounced something. There was quite a pride culture there. But I just tried my best to be pleasant with everybody, and I found that, after a while, when you got to know them, everyone was actually very friendly and we got along well. I started off just as a scientist working in the laboratory, but after a few months they asked me if I would get involved in training other analysts, which was quite a privilege and I was glad to do. I worked in different areas and progressed really well, taking things in and learning quickly, and I like to think I started to prove my worth as a hard-working employee.

In the meantime, the political situation was changing in South Africa. I couldn't believe that just 18 months after I had written my naive piece on that application form, it seemed to be coming true. Everyone was discussing apartheid; you couldn't get away from it. This company was run partly by the government and they could see the way the country was going. My manager was very much an Afrikaans person; he was very tough, didn't speak English and was I think a bit sexist – he didn't generally have much time for women. So I was surprised and delighted when at the end of the first year, he gave me a generous salary increase and a promotion.

But then, during the second half of the year, it happened again. He called me into his office and gave me another salary increase. This was unheard of, particularly from someone like this man. It was only when I left his office that I got to thinking, 'Oh, I get it; this is because of the political situation in South Africa. He thinks he's "doing his bit" for diversity and this has nothing to do with me or my work.'

I felt terrible and very offended. I went storming back into his office. I swear if the salary package had been a tangible thing, I would have thrown it at him! I said to him, 'Look, if this promotion is just to do with politics, then I don't want the job and I don't want the money. I'm not going to be used as a token gesture for this company.'

He looked at me as if I was crazy. He pointed out how hard I had worked during the year, much harder, apparently, than any of my peers. Not convinced, I made him prove to me why he was promoting me. I was lucky he didn't change his mind!

Looking back, that event was quite an historic moment for me. I was in the wrong, I know, because I had jumped to conclusions. But it was the first time in my life that I had really evaluated who I am and where I am and what my beliefs are. I knew I wanted to progress in this field but I wanted it to be because of my work and my merits, not my race.

Source: Sunetha Diaram, story-gathering interview.

Reflection

This story could be used for:

Emotional intelligence (understanding self and others).

Empowerment/engagement.

Equality and diversity.

Motivation and reward.

Self-belief.

Talking points

What experiences have you had where you have found yourself in the minority – whether in terms of race, gender, level of knowledge, etc?

How did this make you feel?

How did you deal with these feelings?

Was Sunetha right or wrong to challenge the promotion?

Might there be someone in your organization who has felt this way because of similar circumstances?

14 Remember the small things

Mother Teresa, born in Albania in 1910, cared for the sick, homeless and dying for over 40 years. She became an international living legend, and received the Nobel Peace prize in 1979. Here she tells the story of what she saw as a small act of kindness.

Some of my sisters work in Australia. On a reservation, among the Aborigines, there was an elderly man. I can assure you that you have never seen a situation as difficult as that poor old man's. He was completely ignored by everyone. His home was disordered and dirty. I told him, 'Please, let me clean your house, wash your clothes and make your bed.' He answered, 'I'm okay like this. Let it be.'

I said again, 'You will be still better if you allow me to do it.' He finally agreed. So I was able to clean his house and wash his clothes. I discovered a beautiful lamp, covered with dust. Only God knows how many years had passed since he last lit it. I said to him, 'Don't you light your lamp? Don't you ever use it?'

He answered, 'No. No one comes to see me. I have no need to light it. Who would I light it for?'

I asked, 'Would you light it every night if the sisters came?' He replied, 'Of course.'

From that day on the sisters committed themselves to visiting him every evening. We cleaned the lamp, and the sisters would light it every evening. Two years passed. I had completely forgotten that man. He sent this message: 'Tell my friend that the light she lit in my life continues to shine still.' I thought it was a very small thing. We need to remember the small things.

Reference: Mother Teresa (1997) *In the Heart of the World*, New World Library, Novato, CA.

Reflection

Never underestimate seemingly small acts of kindness. They may be perceived as life-changing by the person who receives them.

This story could be used for:

Emotional intelligence (understanding self and others).

Perceptions.

Positive thinking.

Integrity/humility.

Talking points

Why was the light so important to the man? What did it symbolize?

Was the man right in saying, 'Who would I light it for?'?

What 'small thing' might you do for someone that could be perceived as an act of kindness?

Is kindness of this sort still appropriate in the modern world?

15 Black and white pebbles

A long time ago, in Tibet, there lived a Buddhist monk called Geshe Ben Gungyal. His sole practice was to observe his mind very closely so that he could quell any delusions or negative thoughts whenever they arose. To help him in his practice and gauge his progress, Geshe Ben Gungyal carried with him a pile of black pebbles and a pile of white pebbles. Whenever a negative thought came into his mind, he placed a black pebble in front of him. Whenever a positive, peaceful thought arose, he placed a white pebble in front of him.

At the end of each day, he would count up the pebbles. Some days, there were more black pebbles than white ones; when this happened he would reprimand himself and set a goal to try harder the next day. If there were more white pebbles than black he would praise and encourage himself. At the beginning of his quest, the black pebbles greatly outnumbered the white, but over the months and years, his mind improved to such an extent that he reached the point where whole days went by without there being any black pebbles.

Reference: A retold Buddhist story. The original featured in Geshe Kelsang Gyatso (2000) *Eight Steps to Happiness*, Tharpa Publications, Glen Spey, NY.

Reflection

Very often a tangible and visual sign of one's progress – a chart, a list or a graph – can be a useful tool.
   This story could be used for:

   Empowerment/engagement.

   Realistic goal setting.

   Motivation.

Performance management.

Self-belief.

Talking points

Do you think that the use of the black and white pebbles was a good one?

What measures do you use to chart progress?

Is it necessary to have negative as well as positive measures?

Would you have more black or white pebbles at the end of the day?

16 The power of influence

This extract featured in Daniel Goleman's ground-breaking book, Emotional Intelligence. *I have used it several times in workshops and coaching sessions to illustrate the point that we are all born with an abundance of influencing skills – which over time we tend to lose.*

Five-year-old Len has lost all patience with his younger brother Jay, who is making a mess of the Lego bricks. Pushed to the limit, Len bites Jay, who not surprisingly bursts into tears. Their mother, on hearing Jay's pained cries, hurries over and immediately scolds Len, ordering him to put away the Lego bricks. Len, reacting to what must seem a huge injustice, also bursts into tears – but his mother, still peeved over the event, refuses to console him.

At this point, Jay, although originally the injured party, now becomes so concerned with his older brother's distress that he embarks on a creative campaign to soothe him. 'Stop crying, Len,' he says. 'Stop crying.' But Len still cries. Jay then beseeches their mother on Len's behalf. 'Len crying, Mummy! Len crying. Look. Me show you. Len crying.' Turning to Len, Jay now adopts a mothering mode, patting his weeping brother on the arm and reassuring him in soothing tones, 'Look, Len, no go on crying.'

But Len's sobs continue. Undeterred, Jay adopts a different tactic, lending a helping hand with the offending Lego bricks. 'I put this back for Lennie, hey?' As this attempt also proves futile, the ever-ingenious Jay tries yet another strategy, this time one of distraction. Showing his brother a toy car, he tries to draw his attention away from the Lego. 'What's this, Len? What's this?'

This mini-drama is a good illustration of the remarkable sophistication that a toddler of some thirty months can bring to bear in trying to manage someone else's emotions.

Reference: An extract from Goleman, D (1995) *Emotional Intelligence*, Bloomsbury.

Reflection

We have so many ways of influencing, which as children we use constantly; but as adults we tend to forget them, preferring to resort to the same one or two that usually get the best results. One of the best ways of relearning influencing skills is to observe a child trying to get their own way.

This story could be used for:

Communication.

Influencing.

Perceptions.

Problem solving.

Talking points

What definition of 'influencing' could you glean from the story?

What were the different types of influencing skills demonstrated in the story?

What are your experiences of influencing styles – in children or adults?

What is your preferred influencing style?

How might you or others adopt more flexibility like Jay?

17 The elves and the shoemaker

Originally a tale from the collection of the brothers Grimm, first published in 1812, the message still raises interesting and topical questions about reward and motivation.

Once upon a time, there lived a shoemaker and his wife. The shoemaker was a good and honest man but, through no fault of his own, had fallen on hard times. He was so poor that eventually he had only enough leather to make one final pair of shoes. So that night he cut out the leather for the shoes, saying to his wife, 'I'll get up early in the morning and sew them up. And then, after that ... well, I don't know what we'll do.'

But in the morning, much to his amazement, he was greeted by the finest pair of shoes standing finished on his table. He looked at the shoes – they were beautifully stitched and polished – better than he could have done himself! Soon a wealthy customer came to the shoemaker's shop. 'That's a fine pair of shoes!' he said, seeing them in the window. He was so pleased with them that he paid a handsome price, far more than the shoemaker could usually command. Now the shoemaker had enough money to buy leather for two pairs of shoes. Again, he cut them out, ready to sew up and finish off in the morning. But he did not need to – for sure enough, the following morning, on his table were two pairs of shoes, both beautifully finished just as before. And once again, eager customers came into his shop and, after admiring the shoes, were willing to pay a huge sum for them.

This time, the shoemaker had enough leather for four pairs of shoes. Again, he cut out the leather, saying to his wife, 'I'll sew those up tomorrow.' And again, in the morning, four wonderful pairs of shoes were sitting on his table, waiting to be sold. This went on for some time, and the shoemaker and his wife gradually found themselves out of debt and making a good living again.

One night, the shoemaker said to his wife, 'I'm curious as to who or what is helping us in this way. I would like to thank them for their kindness.' His wife agreed and together they hid in a corner of the room where the shoes were sewn. Nothing happened for some time, then, around midnight, two little naked elves appeared. Without a word, they sat down and busied themselves, stitching and sewing and hammering with their tiny fingers. They didn't stop until everything on the table was finished – and then they ran out of the window and away. The shoemaker and his wife couldn't believe their eyes.

The next day, the shoemaker's wife said, 'We owe so much to those little elves; I would love to do something for them in return. Perhaps I can make them some clothes to keep them warm. I could make each of them a little shirt and some pantaloons and you can make each of them a pair of shoes.' The shoemaker agreed that this was an excellent idea, and together they made the clothes and left them on the table, ready for when the elves came in. And sure enough, at the same time, the two little men appeared, ready to start their work as usual. But when they saw the clothes and the shoes that the kind shoemaker and his wife had made for them, they laughed and danced with glee, quickly putting them on. As they did, they sang:

> 'Now we're boys so fine and neat,
> Why cobble more for others' feet?'

Still laughing, they hopped and skipped straight out of the window. And from that day, the shoemaker and his wife never saw the elves again.

Reference: A retold traditional folk tale from the collection known as *Grimms' Fairy Tales* (or *Grimms Märchen*), written by Jacob and Wilhelm Grimm and first published in 1812.

Reflection

This tale could be used for:

Integrity/humility.

Leadership.

Motivation and reward.

Teamwork.

Talking points

Once rewarded, the elves stopped working. Was it right to reward them?

Some versions of the tale say that the elves found the clothes restricting. Was this the right gift for them?

Should the shoemaker and his wife have relied on the elves in this way?

What lessons did the shoemaker and his wife learn from the elves?

18 Hidden treasures

I first came across a version of this story in an edition of The Power of Now *by Eckhart Tolle, although its message has appeared in different formats over the years.*

An old beggar had been sitting by the side of the road for many years. One day a stranger walked up to him. 'Spare some change?' the beggar asked, optimistically holding out a faded old baseball cap.

'I have nothing to give you,' replied the stranger, 'except ... what is that you're sitting on?' he mused.

'It's nothing,' replied the beggar, bending down to look at his feet. 'It's just an old box; I've been sitting on it for as long as I can remember.'

'What's inside it?' asked the stranger.

'Nothing,' replied the beggar. 'It's empty, I think.'

'So, you've never looked inside it?' queried the stranger. 'Why not have a look?'

'There doesn't seem much point...' replied the beggar; but nevertheless, he bent down and after some initial struggling, managed to prise off the lid. To his astonishment, the box was filled with gold.

Reference: Retold story that featured in Tolle, E (2005) *The Power of Now*, Hodder and Stoughton, Sevenoaks, Kent.

Reflection

All of us have qualities that we don't recognize, acknowledge or just don't know are there.

This story could be used for:

Creativity.

Emotional intelligence (understanding self and others).

Empowerment/engagement.

Self-belief.

Talent management.

Talking points

What does the story mean to you?

What 'box' have you or others you know been sitting on?

Does everyone have hidden treasures?

What might stop you or others from looking in the box?

Could there be any disadvantages of opening the box?

19 The princess and the pea

This is one of the shortest but best-known tales by Hans Christian Andersen, first published in 1835. It may have been inspired by Andersen's own preoccupation with the inequalities of class, and certainly prompted some mixed reactions from his readers.

Once there was a prince who wanted to marry a princess – but she had to be a real princess. He searched all over the world and met many beautiful, talented women, but there was always something wrong with each of them – and none of them seemed to him to be a genuine, authentic princess. And so each time, he returned home wearily, and was very sad.

Then one stormy night, as the wind howled and the rain beat down relentlessly all around the castle, there was a knock at the door – quite timid at first, but then becoming louder and more insistent. The old king went to open it and standing there, very wet and bedraggled from the rain, was a young woman.

'Please can you give me shelter from the storm?' she pleaded with the king. The king took pity on the girl, and welcomed her into the castle. The girl claimed to be a princess, but the queen, on hearing her say this, said to herself, 'We'll soon find out if that is true.' She went into the bedroom that they had offered the princess, and stripping down the bed, laid a single pea on the bedstead, and then covered it up with 20 mattresses and 20 featherbeds.

In the morning, the queen asked her guest how she had slept. 'Oh, dreadfully!' said the princess. 'There was something in the bed that was so uncomfortable, I couldn't sleep a wink. And look, I am black and blue all over.' Now the king and queen knew without a doubt that this was a real princess, as no one else would have such delicate skin and have the sensitivity to feel the pea underneath all the bedclothes.

So the prince, overjoyed that he had at last found a real princess, took her to be his wife – and the pea was taken and put into a museum for all to see, which goes to prove that this is a true story.

Reference: A retold traditional fairy tale written by Hans Christian Andersen and first published in Danish in 1835.

Reflection

In these times when emotional intelligence is cited as a requirement for a good leader, can we be oversensitive to situations?

This story could be used for:

Integrity/humility.

Emotional intelligence (understanding self and others).

Equality and diversity.

Perceptions.

Talking points

Was the princess's reaction to the pea an indication of her warmth and compassion – or of something else?

Was the 'pea' test a reliable one? Could there have been another explanation for the young woman's reaction?

Was the queen right to test the princess?

Are there times when this degree of sensitivity is not a good thing?

20 Is that it?

On 13 July 1985, the Live Aid concert, organized by Bob Geldof and Midge Ure, was held in London and Philadelphia in aid of famine relief in Ethiopia. It was attended by some 82,000 people in the UK and 100,000 in the USA and was one of the greatest assemblies of rock musicians ever. In his autobiography, Geldof sums up the final moments of the day:

On the day of the Live Aid concert, at the end of 17 hours of live music which had been watched by more people than any other event in history, Bill Graham, the promoter in the US, stepped out onto the stage in Philadelphia. It was 11 pm. In London I stepped out of the nightclub where I had watched the final section of the biggest concert the world had ever seen. It was 4 am. For both of us there was a sense of triumph.

'I did it,' I thought.

'That was unbelievable,' thought Bill, 3,000 miles away.

In Philadelphia they were sweeping the stage. In London they were sweeping the streets. Around both of us were the last remnants of the mighty crowd. As I climbed into my taxi, Bill walked down to look at the emptying stadium. Just in front of the stage were a group of kids, hanging around, still finishing what was left of their beer.

One of them turned to him and shouted, 'Hey you, Bill Graham.'

Bill looked down with an enquiring smile.

The kid shouted up. 'Is that it?'

It's something I keep asking myself.

Reference: Extract from Geldof, B (1986) *Is That It?*, Sidgwick & Jackson Ltd, London.

Reflection

The inference of the story is that the fight against poverty and disease is never-ending.

This story could be used for:

Problem solving.

Dealing with change.

Leadership.

Project management.

Talking points

Was the boy asking if the concert had ended – or was he referring to the end of something else?

After seeing the biggest concert ever, the boy sounds somewhat dismissive. Is there a danger of raising expectations through giving people too much?

Can problems like the ones Geldof was facing be 'solved', or will they be for ever recurring?

Why does Geldof say, 'It's something I keep asking myself'?

CAUTIONARY TALES

This second collection of tales is intended to educate and warn against certain threats or perceived dangers. The cautionary tale by its very nature often had a less-than-happy ending – indeed its role was to shock the listener out of complacency. These 20 stories – that include the wisdom of traditional fairy tales and modern tales of woe from the shop floor – can serve as a useful focus for group discussion or as a vehicle for knowledge sharing.

The stories can be used to cover such topics as: dealing with change, problem solving, project management, talent management, teamwork, customer service, perceptions, integrity and humility.

21 The goose that laid the golden eggs

I used this tale with a large retailing organization in Ireland who were debating the future direction of the company, and considering, particularly during a recession, whether too much money was being spent on marketing and development – or not enough.

Once there was a poor farmer who lived with his wife in a little ramshackle cottage. They had between them just a few sheep and a few goats – and a pet goose. One day, when the farmer went to collect the eggs that the goose had laid, he found, instead of an ordinary egg, one that was made of solid gold. The farmer looked at the egg, looked at the goose and looked around him. 'This must be some sort of trick,' he said, and called to his wife, 'Wife! Come quickly and look at this!' The farmer's wife came out to see what the fuss was about. 'The goose has laid a golden egg!' said the farmer. The farmer's wife looked at the egg, looked at the goose and looked at the farmer. 'This must be some sort of trick,' she said. 'Why don't we take the egg into the village and ask the goldsmith to look at it?'

The goldsmith confirmed that the egg was indeed gold and offered the farmer and his wife a good price for it, more money than they had ever had in their lives. The following day, the farmer went out again to see the goose. And sure enough, the goose had laid another golden egg, bigger and shinier even than the one before. The farmer couldn't wait to take the second egg into the village, where he was offered twice as much money as the day before. Every day after that, the goose laid a golden egg, and the farmer and his wife became fabulously wealthy. They moved out of their little ramshackle cottage and into a splendid mansion. They wore not peasant clothes but the latest and best fashion that money could buy. They hired a number of farm workers who could do the heavy work for them on the farm, while they sat around eating and drinking with their newly found friends.

All this time, the goose carried on laying golden eggs. But then one day the farmer's wife said, 'Do you know, I think that goose is getting too fat. Look at it; it can hardly waddle around the yard. It makes the place look untidy. And anyway, we're spending too much on animal feed. I shall tell the girl to cut its rations.' And so the goose was fed leftover scraps from the other animals; it started to get thinner and thinner – and the eggs got smaller and smaller.

One day the farmer's wife said, 'That goose is getting to look really ugly. And it's not laying half as many eggs as it used to. We can hardly scrape by on what it produces. But I've got a good idea. Why don't we kill it and open it up? Then we can get all the golden eggs in one go rather than having to wait – *and* we don't have to feed the goose any more. Think what we'll save!' 'Great idea!' said the farmer, and without further ado, he took his axe and chopped off the goose's head.

The foolish pair looked eagerly inside the goose's body, hoping to discover a hoard of golden eggs. But there were no golden eggs – inside it was just like any other goose. The farmer and his wife looked at the goose and then looked at each other. Too late they realized that now there would be no more golden eggs, for they had destroyed the goose that produced them.

Reference: A retold story. The original featured in Lord, J V and Michie, J (1989), *Aesop's Fables*, Jonathan Cape, London.

Reflection

Be careful not to destroy the very thing that is providing you with your good fortune.

This story could be used for:

Leadership.

Project management.

Strategic planning.

Realistic goal setting.

Branding/marketing.

Talking points

This is a cautionary tale. What vices does the story caution against?

What did the man and his wife learn?

Can you relate this story to your own or others' experiences?

How might the tale have had a happy ending – or was it a happy ending anyway?

22 Premature birth

Stories and symbols using caterpillars and butterflies appear frequently in the world of business storytelling. Their natural progression seems a good metaphor for organizational and individual growth. I have used this story to illustrate the dangers of pushing learning or change too quickly.

One day a man, walking around his garden, found the cocoon of a butterfly. As he watched it, a small opening appeared. Mesmerized, he sat and watched it for several hours as it struggled to force its body through the little hole. It got so far – and then stopped. It looked for all the world like it had given up struggling.

The man decided he couldn't just stand by and watch the apparent demise of the exhausted butterfly, so he took a pair of scissors and snipped off the remaining bit of the cocoon that seemed to be giving the emerging insect such a problem. Sure enough, the butterfly then emerged easily. But to the man's disappointment, it had a large, swollen body and wings that looked shrivelled up. As the man continued to watch the butterfly, he felt sure that in time a colourful pair of wings would emerge and expand on either side of the ugly body, which would then shrink to a normal butterfly size.

But sadly, neither of these things happened. In fact, the butterfly spent the rest of its life crawling around with its oversized body and its shrivelled-up wings. It never was able to fly and died soon afterwards. The man, in his well-meant act of kindness, did not appreciate how the struggle required for the butterfly to get through the tiny opening was in fact a necessary part of the process. The action forced fluid from the body of the butterfly into its wings so that it would be ready for flight once it achieved its freedom.

Source: Anecdotal, unknown author.

Reflection

The story illustrates the dangers of lack of patience and understanding, which had catastrophic effects for the butterfly.

This story could be used for:

Learning and development.

Dealing with change.

Problem solving.

Talent management.

Talking points

How could the story of the butterfly relate to people's development within your organization?

In a business context, what are the consequences of forcing change or development? Are they good or bad?

The man's actions turned out to have a negative impact – but was his motivation positive or negative?

23 Black spot and green slime

I am indebted to trainer Michael Astrop, who is himself a great advocate of stories and storytelling, for passing on this sadly all-too-common type of tale. See more on knowledge sharing in Chapter 1.

I had been asked by a printing-plate manufacturer to develop a problem-solving process for their production line, as they continually had blemishes or marks occurring during the plate-coating process. The solving of these problems was taking some considerable time and every time a blemish or mark occurred the whole continuous production line stopped, thereby causing some considerable cost. It was worse on the night shift, although the day shift was also badly affected.

I started by monitoring the production-line process and waited for one of these blemishes or marks to occur. Shortly after I started my observation the hooter sounded and the line stopped. I went over to the operator, looked at the plate and said, 'What is it?' to which he replied, 'Black spot.' I then asked naively, 'How do you know that?' to which he replied with the tone of a man used to idiots, 'It's black and it's a spot!' I came to realize that they had a descriptive name for every chemical manifestation that occurred, from 'white mist' to 'green slime'.

My next question to the operator was, 'What do you do when you identify the mark?' and again with a sigh he said, 'Report it to the supervisor and they go away and then come back and tell us what to do differently.' 'Even on nights?' I asked and an affirmative response was forthcoming. I then asked, 'Do the supervisors show you what they have done (it was usually a chemical rebalance of the film mixture) and do you make a note of the treatment for each mark for future reference?' A swift response in the consistent tone of voice left me in no doubt as to the process: 'No!'

My next port of call was the supervisor's office; I recalled my conversation with the operator and the supervisor confirmed that the procedure as outlined was correct. I then asked, 'How do you know the treatment for each mark or blemish?' The swift reply came back: 'We have a book.' He then promptly brought out a handwritten tome from a locked cabinet and on opening it I saw 'Black spot', 'Green slime' and many more, each with the prescription for solving the chemical imbalance. With some hesitation I said, 'Why don't you let the operators have a copy of this book?' The supervisor looked scathingly at me and said, 'Then they would know what we know.'

Source: Michael Astrop's website: www.coachthemind.com.

Reflection

In some organizations there is still a resistance to knowledge sharing. Knowledge can still be perceived as a manipulative tool of power, rather than as something which might be used for the greater good.

This story could be used for:

Knowledge sharing.

Learning and development.

Leadership.

Talent management.

Teamwork.

Talking points

Is knowledge sharing encouraged in your organization?

Are you stopping someone else progressing with new learning?

Is your perception that information is shared with the privileged few?

Is acquisition of knowledge seen as a benefit for the organization as a whole or for personal power?

24 For the want of a nail

I used this poem on a workshop where the company was debating the importance of customer care. Having discussed the meaning of the poem, the participants later had great fun with an exercise that I loosely based on the parlour game 'Consequences', where each person writes a comment and passes it on to the next. There were some rather irreverent observations, but it got the point across!

> For want of a nail the shoe was lost.
> For want of a shoe the horse was lost.
> For want of a horse the rider was lost.
> For want of a rider the battle was lost.
> For want of a battle the kingdom was lost.
> And all for the want of a horseshoe nail.

Reference: Unconfirmed source. A traditional tale quoted, among others, by Benjamin Franklin in his *Poor Richard's Almanack* of 1758, and thought originally to date back to the 14th century.

Reflection

The poem highlights the dangers of ignoring what might seem to be a small action, as rather large and nasty consequences can arise. The poem is a good example of what is also referred to as the 'butterfly' effect or chaos theory and illustrates the need for everyone to accept responsibility.

This poem could be used for:

Project management.

Strategic planning.

Dealing with change.

Customer service.

Leaders and teams.

Talking points

Can you relate the message of the story to your own situation or that of others in your organization?

What situations have you experienced where the 'kingdom' was lost because of a small oversight?

Causal chains like this tend only to be seen in hindsight. Is there a way of preventing such a chain developing?

25 The vain prince

This is a traditional tale from India, from the Jainism religion, which is also sometimes called Jain Dharma. The other various Indian religions, such as Hinduism and Buddhism, advocate following dharma (law or teaching) towards a spiritual path, and make much use of stories to encourage learning.

There was once a young prince who was besotted with his own beauty. If any traveller came to the palace he would ask them, 'Have you ever seen anyone as handsome as me?' Not surprisingly no one ever had. A particularly obsequious traveller even said to him, 'I don't think there could be anyone in the whole world as good-looking as you. I don't think even a god could be as handsome.' This made the prince very happy and he went around telling everyone that he was more handsome than the gods. Hearing his boast and angered by the young prince's vanity, two gods came to the palace.

'We have come to see if you are as handsome as you claim,' they said.

'And aren't I?' asked the vain prince, looking into his mirror.

'You are indeed handsome, Sire,' said the first god. 'But not as handsome as you were when we looked on you earlier in the day.'

'No indeed,' said the second god. 'And definitely not as handsome as when we saw you yesterday and you were still asleep.'

The young prince was horrified. 'Do you mean my looks have declined in just a few hours?' he cried. 'How can that be?'

'All mortal things change and decline with age, your majesty,' said one of the gods. 'Bring us a bowl of water and we will prove it to you.'

A bowl of water was duly brought in. The first god asked the prince to study it closely and then leave the room. When the prince had done this, the second god very carefully removed half a spoonful of water from the bowl. Then they called the prince back in.

'Now look carefully, your majesty, at the bowl of water,' said the first god. 'Do you see any change in it?'

'None,' said the prince.

'And yet the water has diminished,' said the second god, showing the spoon, 'just in the same way that your beauty has deteriorated.'

The prince was beside himself with grief. But after a while, when he started to calm and reflect on what the gods had taught him, he said, 'I understand that my looks, and indeed everyone's, are diminishing day by day. Beauty is indeed short-lived. Why then am I so attached to something that is so fleeting? I should concern myself with that which is meaningful and eternal.'

After that day, the young prince never again looked into a mirror and in the course of time he renounced his throne and was ordained as a monk.

Reference: Retold story that features in www.dimdima.com.

Reflection

The tale illustrates how imperceptible the stages of change can be (either good or bad) and warns us of the perils of becoming attached to transient things.

This story could be used for:

Dealing with change.

Emotional intelligence (understanding self and others).

Integrity/humility.

Perceptions.

Talking points

Was the prince wrong to have such self-belief?

What did he learn from the experience?

What transient things do we become attached to in the business world?

Does the story mean that we shouldn't have or want beautiful things?

26 Narcissus and Echo

Most people have heard of Narcissus and Echo, although they may not be aware of the tale's origins from the Greek myths – a very poignant little tale about unrequited love and arrogance.

Echo was a nymph whose constant chatter and storytelling sufficiently distracted the goddess Hera that her husband Zeus found plenty of time for affairs. When Hera discovered the deception, she took away Echo's voice, allowing her only to repeat others' words.

Echo fell in love with a beautiful youth called Narcissus. Every boy and girl in the town was in love with him, and yet he spurned them all. Echo followed him everywhere, hopelessly unable to proclaim her love. One day he went hunting in the woods and, aware that he was being followed, shouted, 'Who is there?'

'There!' replied the lovelorn Echo.

'Come here,' shouted Narcissus.

'Here!' replied Echo, running to embrace her love. But Narcissus, being a vain and shallow creature, pushed her away. 'Leave me alone!' he shouted.

'Alone!' replied the heartbroken Echo.

Now the goddess of retribution, Nemesis, had witnessed this unhappy scene, and furious with Narcissus's callous treatment of the nymph, decided to punish him. Soon after, Narcissus lay down by the side of a pool in order to drink. In doing so, he saw his own reflection for the first time, and fell madly in love with the beautiful boy, not realizing it was indeed himself. Time after time, he bent into the water to kiss the reflection, and eventually, becoming so obsessed with his apparently unrequited love, became weaker and weaker and eventually died. As he died, his body disappeared, leaving in its place a beautiful white flower. To this day, the narcissus flower stands on the edge of the water, so that it can lean over and gaze at its own reflection.

Reference: A retold Greek myth.

Reflection (no pun intended)

The story goes that Narcissus's mother consulted a prophet regarding her son's future. The prophet told her that Narcissus would live to a ripe old age, 'if he didn't to know himself'. In some versions of the tale Narcissus does realize that the beautiful image is in fact himself – and he dies of grief with the realization that his love can never be returned in the way he desires.

This story could be used for:

Perceptions.

Communication.

Emotional intelligence (understanding of self and others).

Integrity/humility.

Talking points

What is meant by the expression 'come to know yourself'?

Is it a good or bad thing to 'know yourself' in today's society?

Was Narcissus arrogant or ignorant – or both?

Was Nemesis's punishment of him justified?

27 Monkey business

People in organizations very quickly learn the 'right' behaviour in order to be accepted by their peers. This true story might explain why and how that happens.

A scientist studying animal behaviour positions three monkeys in a line in an animal cage. Hanging above the third monkey is a juicy bunch of bananas. Naturally the third monkey instinctively reaches to grab a banana, at which point his two fellows are drenched with water. Somewhat angered by this, the two attack the third monkey, but he hasn't really made the connection and continues to reach for bananas – and every time he does, the other two get a soaking.

At this point, the scientist steps into the cage, removes the third monkey and replaces him with a new monkey. His reaction is the same: he spots the lovely bananas – but this time, as soon as he stretches out his arm, he is attacked by the other two monkeys. Of course, this makes no sense at all to the new monkey, but he quickly learns to stop going after the bananas.

Some time passes, and the scientist again intervenes – this time to remove one of the drenched monkeys and replace him with a new one. This new monkey again goes for the bananas and the other two attack him. Then the scientist replaces the final one of the original monkeys with a new one. This new monkey is immediately attacked by the other two – even when the banana–water system has been turned off – and of course he has no idea why.

The scientist keeps repeating the experiment, and even with the water turned off, any new monkey that is introduced into the cage is attacked by the other two.

Reference: Anecdotal, source unknown.

Reflection

The story demonstrates the power of learning and how culture is very quickly and effectively passed down from one generation to the next, very often without question.

This story could be used for:

Dealing with change.

Learning and development.

Motivation and reward.

Talking points

What is the moral of the story?

How do people in your organization learn what is 'acceptable' behaviour?

Is certain behaviour condoned without question?

What does the story tell you about motivation and reward?

What does the story tell you about the power of negative reinforcement?

28 Mother's special voice

My mother, like many of us, had a 'special' refined voice that she reserved for job interviews, conversations with other refined ladies who came to tea in the afternoon and persistent salesmen on the telephone. The 'voice' made some words almost unrecognizable – for example the word 'and' was drawn out to become 'yandaah', 'hello' became 'hellaaaar'. And sometimes it could backfire ... as the story shows.

Mother was tall and slim, with a naturally elegant stature, enhanced by the fact that she very often wore her hair up in a bun and smoked (in the days when it was still allowed) a cigarette through a very long and stylish cigarette holder. Having had the family (ie me and my sister), she made the decision to return to teaching, something of a rarity in those days when the majority of women gave up work on having children. So Mother felt the need to prove (to herself as much as to anyone else) her capability in doing the job. When she was told that an inspector of schools was due to assess her teaching, she was naturally apprehensive and eager to impress. With clipboard in hand, the inspector approached Mother in the classroom.

'And what is your specialist subject, Mrs Fletcher? What are we teaching here this morning?' he crooned.

Mother thought it best to try and disguise the possibly odd mixture of Scottish and Yorkshire dialect that she had accumulated since marrying, and so replied using her very best 'special' voice, slowly and deliberately, in a tone that would have been the envy of Greta Garbo.

'I am teaching English ... yandaaah ... Maths, Mr McGregor,' she said, in such a way that the vowel sounds were lengthened almost to a drawl, in particular the last word: 'M–a–w–t–h–s'.

'How fascinating,' replied the inspector, smiling. 'I don't think I've ever met anyone in school before who specialized in lepidoptery.'

Smiling and nodding in return at his reaction, but with no idea of the significance of the conversation, Mother did her best to retain her confident and composed manner for the rest of the lesson.

It was only later, after the inspector had left the school, that she was able to run to the staffroom to consult the dictionary, and discover, to her horror, that 'lepidoptery' is the study of moths and butterflies.

Source: Family story.

Reflection

This story could be used for:

Communication.

Self-belief.

Integrity/humility.

Influence.

Talking points

Was Mother being true to herself?

Should she have confessed her error to the inspector?

What situations have you come across where trying to be someone you're not has got you into trouble?

People say the best way of dealing with a tense situation is to 'just be yourself' – is this good advice?

29 The fox and the grapes

I find that even those who don't know its origins are still familiar with the term 'sour grapes'. The original version of the fable was reputedly written by the Greek slave Aesop, in the mid 6th century BC.

It was a hot summer's day, and a hungry fox, walking down the lane, saw a bunch of the juiciest-looking grapes, hanging just out of reach on a branch above her.

'Those would be just the thing to quench my thirst,' thought the fox. 'I can almost taste them.' And she started to drool in anticipation. With a run and a jump she sprang as high as she could – but just missed the branch. Undeterred, she tried again, running a bit harder and jumping a bit higher – but still the branch was out of reach. Time and again, the fox tried with all her might to reach that elusive vine – but to no avail. She just could not jump high enough to reach them. Eventually, exhausted, the fox decided to give up the effort. Walking away from the grapes, she said to herself,

'I didn't really want those grapes anyway – they looked sour.'

Reference: Retold tale. The original featured in Lord, J V and Michie, J (1989), *Aesop's Fables*, Jonathan Cape, London.

Reflection

The moral of the fable is that it is easy to despise what you cannot have. In psychology, this strategy is known as 'rationalization' or 'cognitive dissonance' – where we deal with our disappointment by devaluing the object that we once desired.

This story could be used for:

Perceptions.

Realistic goal setting.

Positive thinking.

Self-belief.

Talking points

Is 'sour grapes' a good or bad practice to adopt?

What might the positive outcomes of this strategy be?

Is this an honest policy?

Are there situations when it might not be a useful strategy?

What might have been a different ending to the story?

30 The woman who lived with Fear

There are a number of stories, poems and songs where emotions are personified or given solid substance. In Shakespeare's Othello, *Iago refers to jealousy as the 'green-eyed monster'; in the sixties the Walker Brothers sang about loneliness as 'the cloak you wear'. In the case of a negative emotion, such as fear, the personification can help to diminish the strength of the feeling.*

She never knew why Fear came to live with her – but he seemed to be with her constantly, so much so that she would not venture out of her house, or see her friends or talk to strangers. One day she decided, 'I will go outside and meet with my friends.' But she only got as far as the door when Fear stood in her way, towering over her and laughing, saying, 'You will never go out; just think what might happen. If you met people you didn't know, they might belittle you and make fun of you. Besides, see how bad the weather is; you may catch your death of cold. Best not to go.'

The woman listened, and although she tried to argue, in the end she decided to agree with Fear. The next day she got up, thinking, 'Today I will go outside and walk in the sun.' But once again at the door she was stopped in her tracks by Fear. This time she wrestled with him in an attempt to get to the door. But after hours of struggling she was exhausted, and in the end decided not to go.

The next day, she got up, thinking, 'Today I will go outside and pick some flowers.' This time, when she got to the door, Fear was waiting as usual, but this time he didn't look quite so intimidating and she caught him off guard. Knocking him off balance, she pushed him over and ran through the door. She had a wonderful day, meeting her friends, picking flowers and walking in the sun, so much so, that she did it the next day, and the day after that – and never gave Fear another thought. Indeed, Fear seemed to have vanished altogether.

But then on the fourth day, while walking through the woods, she suddenly saw a huge bear, running straight towards her, snarling and growling. She stood for a moment, transfixed with terror. Then, apparently out of nowhere, Fear stepped up and grabbed her by the hand, pulling her along and helping her to run and run and run, so fast that eventually she managed to escape from the bear.

Once back home, Fear said, 'I told you something bad like this would happen to you if you went outside. Perhaps now you'll listen to me.'

And the woman did – and in the morning, when she awoke, there was Fear standing just as large and menacing by the doorway. Somewhat timidly she approached him and said, 'Fear, why have you become so large and menacing again?'

Fear replied, 'You must learn to deal with me every day. And you must learn the difference between when you need me and when you don't.'

'Ah, now I understand,' said the woman, and as soon as she had uttered these words, Fear shrank to the size of a tiny dwarf sitting cross-legged on the floor. On seeing this, she picked him up and put him carefully in her pocket.

She never knew why Fear came to live with her. But now she is happy to carry him round in her pocket, knowing that she can call on him whenever he is needed.

Reference: Retold story, adapted from www.pkal.org.com.

Reflection

This story could be used for:

Self-belief.

Motivation and reward.

Dealing with conflict.

Positive thinking.

Talking points

Is it a useful ploy to personify a negative emotion such as fear?

What are the benefits/disadvantages of doing this?

In what situations might you find this strategy useful?

Is it right to carry fear in your pocket?

31 | WarGames

The film WarGames *was produced over 25 years ago. I've seen it several times, but I must admit that I always enjoy watching it. Although essentially it is a children's adventure, like many before it the story contains some powerful cautionary (and timeless) messages that are probably just as relevant to adults.*

Young underachieving student and amateur computer hacker, David Lightman, in a search for the latest computer game, accidentally taps into the United States military's supercomputer War Operations Plan Response, or WOPR, whose purpose is to run simulations of possible outcomes of nuclear war. David, quite unwittingly and thinking he is playing a game with the computer, suggests that he and WOPR play 'Global Thermonuclear War'.

Of course, the simulation throws the authorities into panic and causes a national nuclear missile scare. When they realize that WOPR is just running a simulation, they attempt to defuse the situation by removing the phone line and 'backdoor password' that David has discovered.

However, unknown to the military executives, WOPR continues to run the simulation in an attempt to trigger the scenario and win the game.

The climax of the plot comes, and disaster is narrowly avoided, when David and the original designer of the computer teach WOPR to play tic–tac–toe (noughts and crosses), from which WOPR learns that the game, just like its many simulations of war, has the same outcome: '*winner – none*'.

Eventually, all permutations exhausted, WOPR concludes, in its disembodied voice: 'This – is – a – strange – game. The only winning move is not – to – play.'

There is a short silence, after which the computer rallies with the suggestion, 'How about a – nice – game – of – chess?'

Reference: *WarGames* was produced in 1983, written by Lawrence Lasker and Walter F. Parkes and directed by John Badham.

Reflection

The last time I saw this film on television (in the summer of 2009) it was followed with a news article featuring the war in Afghanistan. The speaker, Gordon Brown, Prime Minister of the day, was urging that 'the war in Afghanistan must continue'. Perhaps he should have been introduced to WOPR.

This story could be used for:

Dealing with change.

Dealing with conflict.

Perceptions.

Problem solving.

Talking points

Did WOPR come to the right conclusion?

Does engaging in conflict never have a winner?

What 'games' are played in organizations that have no winners or losers?

How could people in organizations learn this lesson?

Is it feasible 'not to play'?

32 Poverty and wisdom

The mullah Nasrudin made his money by standing in the street, to be pointed out as an idiot. When passers-by stood and laughed at him, they would offer him a large and a small coin. Nasrudin would always take the smaller piece. One day, a man, feeling sorry for Nasrudin, said, 'Mullah, you should take the bigger coin. Then you will make more money, and what's more, people won't think of you as an idiot.'

'You're right,' said Nasrudin. 'But then if I were always to take the larger coin, people would no longer think of me as an idiot, and then they would stop offering me money to prove that I am more foolish than them. Then I would have no money at all.'

Reference: A much-told Nasrudin story. More stories are available from the author Idries Shah at www.idriesshah.com.

Reflection

Was Nasrudin the idiot, or were those who gave him money idiots; or was his adviser the idiot?

This tale could be used for:

Branding/marketing.

Perceptions.

Integrity/humility.

Influence.

Talking points

We might say that Nasrudin 'knew his place' in relation to his public. Is the same true in your organization?

Should Nasrudin have taken the man's advice?

What might have happened if he had?

Was his behaviour, begging from others, ethical?

33 The dog and the bone

Another well-known Aesop fable, cautioning against the vices of greed, arrogance and ignorance.

There was once a dog who used to love to sit outside the butcher's shop, and drool at all the chops and sausages and steaks in the window. One day, when the butcher was busy with a customer, the dog spotted his chance and ran into the shop to grab a large ham bone. Off he ran down the street, the ham bone firmly between his teeth, with the butcher running after him, brandishing his sharpest knife and shouting, 'Thief, thief, bring that back!' The dog could run faster than the man, who eventually ran out of steam, and the dog was soon nearly home.

'How clever I am,' the dog thought to himself. 'No one has a bone as big as this. I shall be the talk of the village.'

But as he crossed the bridge near to his home, what should he see in the river but another dog with a bone, just as big as his own.

'My lucky day,' thought the dog. 'Now I can have that bone as well!'

And with that, he opened his mouth and snapped greedily at the reflection. But, instead of having another bone to chew on, he lost the first bone, which fell from his mouth – splash – into the water and sank.

Reference: A retold story. The original featured in Lord, J V and Michie, J (1989), *Aesop's Fables*, Jonathan Cape, London.

Reflection (no pun intended here either!)

This story could be used for:

Realistic goal setting.

Emotional intelligence (understanding self and others).

Integrity/humility.

Talking points

Was this a case of greed or just ignorance on the part of the dog?

Should the dog not be applauded for his ambitious venture?

Was the dog's behaviour ethical?

How might you relate the moral to your organization or others you know?

34 It makes you think

On the day of Princess Diana's funeral, journalists were roaming through the thousands of grieving spectators who were lined up and waiting to see the cortège pass by in order to pay their respects. One journalist approached an elderly couple, standing by the railing.

'Excuse me, Madam,' said the journalist, addressing the woman. 'What do you think about the role of the royal family here today? Should the Queen have come down from Balmoral sooner?' He held the microphone up to her face. The woman stood, motionless and vacant, but then started to giggle nervously.

'Oooh, I don't really know, dear,' she said. Then, turning to her husband standing at her side, she prodded him and said, 'Arthur, what do I think?'

Source: BBC TV interview.

Reflection

This story could be used for:

Communication.

Self-belief.

Equality and diversity.

Empowerment/engagement.

Positive thinking.

Talking points

What was your reaction to the woman's comment to her husband?

This was an elderly couple who were interviewed. Could you imagine this happening in relationships today?

Was the elderly woman right to rely so heavily on her husband?

In what situations might you or others allow other people to think for you?

35 Dilemma tales

These short stories, also sometimes known as 'Judgement tales', and very often of African origin, can be useful in a learning context to help elicit individuals' beliefs, thoughts and values. Their endings are intentionally open to conjecture or are morally ambiguous, and they encourage the audience to comment or speculate on what they see as the 'correct' solution to the problem posed in the tale. Of course, there are no correct answers – at least none will be given here. Typical issues tend to be around conflict of loyalty, deciding who should take responsibility for certain misdemeanours, or having to choose a response to a difficult situation. Here are a couple to whet your appetite.

The doctor's dilemma

A young doctor working in a hospital discovers that he has the power to cure anyone under the age of 70 of any sickness or injury simply by touching them. Any contact, however brief, between any part of his skin and the skin of the patient will cure the disease. He wants to use his gift to benefit humanity. However, he knows that the gift is non-transferable, will last for his lifetime only, and will not persist in tissue separated from his body. The questions are: How should the doctor go about using his gift? How would he choose the patient/s to save? What negative outcomes might there be from the gift?'

Reference: John McCarthy, Professor Emeritus of Computer Science at Stanford University.

The travellers' dilemma

A carpenter, a tailor and a magician go travelling together. They take shelter together in a cave, and to while away the hours, they make a woman out of wood, dress her up, and, finally, give her the breath of life. The question then arises: who should have the woman to be his wife – the carpenter who crafted her, the tailor who clothed her or the magician who gave her life?

Reference: Adapted from www.alanirvine.com.

36 Carly's story

Carly Read is managing director of highly successful IconLive, a jewellery and concessions company operating from the south of England, with its products available in stores and supermarkets worldwide. During a storytelling workshop that I ran recently for her and colleagues, I asked them if any personal stories stood out in their minds as providing valuable lessons for learning. This was Carly's response.

It was 1986, a tough year in retail for everybody. We had already lost one of our big accounts because they didn't want to stock jewellery any more. I had an employee at that time, her name was Ann. She was on the concessions side of the business; it was a responsible job, but I knew from day one that she was a slacker as far as work was concerned. It was a regular occurrence that she would try and stretch her lunch hour into two. She would have her evening newspaper semi-hidden in her desk drawer, which she would deftly elbow shut whenever I passed by her office. She thought I didn't notice, but I knew what was going on. I suppose in my naivety at the time I didn't want to cause an upset, because we were undergoing business problems. I didn't want to have to face her with her slackness. That's an action I bitterly regret.

It was probably a month or so later, when I had to carry out the hardest job of my life, and tell my staff that a number of them would have to be made redundant. It was a poignant moment when, after I had made the announcement, Ann, who was one of those redundant, came up to me and said, looking at me very apologetically and sincerely, 'If only I had known the company was in difficulties, I would have tried harder.'

It was a salutary lesson for me. Had I faced her with her laziness it would have benefited me as well as her. Today I'm a very, very different business woman. I've learnt a lot and it's taken a lot of lessons to become a strong business person.

Source: Carly Read, story-gathering interview. IconLive website: www.iconlive.com.

Reflection

This story could be used for:

Leadership.

Teamwork.

Dealing with conflict.

Positive thinking.

Self-belief.

Talking points

Should Carly have been more open and honest with her staff as to the state of the company?

Was Carly right or wrong to ignore Ann's behaviour?

Do you think that Ann would have changed had she stayed with the company?

How would you have dealt with Ann?

What situations have you come across where you or others have chosen to ignore poor performance? What were the consequences (good or bad)?

37 The little red hen

This traditional folk tale is a good example of what the folk-tale purists call a 'repetitive' story, ie there are at least three stages with repeats that lend the narrative its feeling of structure. Other examples are 'The gingerbread man' and 'The three little pigs'. 'The little red hen', thought to be of Russian origin, is here given something of an update.

One day as she was scratching around in the farmyard, the little red hen found a grain of wheat. She turned to the other animals in the farmyard and enquired, 'Who will help me plant this grain of wheat?'

'Not I,' said the duck. 'I haven't seen a scoping document for such an activity.'

'Nor I,' said the cat.

'Ditto,' said the dog.

'Very well,' said the little red hen cheerily. 'I will plant it myself.' After some time, the grain of wheat grew up tall and golden, and was ripe enough to cut.

'Who will help me cut the wheat?' asked the little red hen.

'Not I,' said the duck. 'With no risk assessment? I don't think so.'

'Nor I,' said the cat.

'Ditto,' said the dog.

'Not to worry,' said the little red hen happily. 'I will cut it myself.'

When the wheat was cut, the little red hen said to her colleagues, 'Who will help me thresh the wheat?'

'Not I,' said the duck. 'No one has considered how this fits in with any project management plan. And besides, I haven't been trained.'

'Nor I,' said the cat.

'Ditto,' said the dog.

'Right-oh,' said the little red hen resolutely. 'I will thresh it myself.'

When the wheat was all neatly threshed, it was ready to be taken to the mill to be ground into flour. The little red hen said to her colleagues, 'I think I might know the answer to this, but would anyone like to help me take this wheat to the mill for grinding into flour?'

'Not I,' said the duck. 'Who is controlling the cost of transport? And think how difficult it will be to find the mill – I have no SatNav.'

'Nor I,' said the cat.

'Ditto,' said the dog.

'Very well,' sighed the little red hen. 'I will take it myself.'

So she took the wheat to the mill, and after it was ground into beautiful smooth flour, she said, 'Any remote chance of anyone helping me make this flour into bread?'

'Not I,' said the duck, 'unless it is intended to be a prototype that can be tested by the end users before an attempt is made to build the final product. And besides, I haven't been told what quality standards of bread are expected.'

'Nor I,' said the cat.

'Ditto,' said the dog.

'Fine,' said the little red hen, slinging the bag of flour over her shoulder. 'I will bake it myself.' And off she trotted in the direction of the kitchens.

Soon she had made the bread and baked it in the oven. It smelt delicious, and all the other animals, including of course the duck, the cat and the dog, hurried along to see what was on offer.

'Now, who will help me eat this bread?' said the little red hen, waving the carving knife in the air.

'I will!' said the duck.

'Me too!' said the cat.

'Ditto!' said the dog.

'Not so fast,' said the little red hen, pointing the knife somewhat malevolently in their direction. 'I seem to remember that when I asked you for help, none of you lot was interested – for all sorts of spurious reasons.

I've done all the work myself; therefore it only seems fair that I get to eat the bread myself too.'

And without further ado, she started to slice the loaf. The other animals, realizing there was no sense in their hanging around, shuffled off one by one.

'Not a team player,' whinged the duck.

'Selfish,' hissed the cat.

'Well, I suppose I can see her point of view,' reflected the dog.

'Oh shut up!' snapped the duck. 'It's a bit late for you to start having an opinion.'

But the little red hen didn't hear them. She and her chicks were too busy enjoying their breakfast.

Reference: A retold traditional story.

Reflection

The original moral of the story was that those who showed no desire to contribute to an end product did not deserve to enjoy the end product.
    This story could be used for:

Project management.

Teamwork.

Communication.

Motivation and reward.

Talking points

Were the animals' criticisms of the little red hen justified?

Should the little red hen have shared the bread?

Were the animals' comments valid – or merely an excuse to avoid hard work?

Are there situations in your organization where comments such as these are used as obstacles rather than as enablers?

Could people in your organization feel pressured into sharing benefits with others after they have put in all the hard work?

38 The Lord will provide

An old traditional tale outlining the dangers of blind faith.

Once there was a great storm, and an old man found that his house was badly flooded. He sat on his porch and watched the flood waters rising slowly, wondering what action he could take to save his house – and himself. He decided that the best thing to do was to pray, and to trust in the Lord. After some time, a makeshift raft approached, with two of his neighbours in it. 'Get onto the raft!' they shouted, holding out their arms to help him in. 'No, thank you,' the man replied. 'I'm going to stay here and trust in the Lord.'

The water rose a little higher and a little higher, and the man soon had to go up to the top floor of his house to keep dry. After some time, a boat approached the house, and floated up to the window, where the man was anxiously peering out. 'Get into the boat!' the people in the boat shouted. 'There's plenty of room.' 'No, thank you,' replied the man. 'I'm trusting in the Lord.'

The flood waters continued to rise and rise and rise, so much so that the old man was forced onto the roof of his house with just a few of his most precious belongings. After some time, he heard a loud whirring noise, and, looking up, saw a helicopter approaching, lowering its ladder and beckoning him to climb up. 'No, thank you,' shouted the man to the men in the helicopter. 'I'm trusting in the Lord.'

Eventually, the violence of the floods proved too much for the old man, and he was swept away in the torrent and drowned. When he reached heaven, the man asked God: 'Lord, I trusted in you and prayed and prayed. Why didn't you come and save me from the floods?'

'But I did,' replied the Lord. 'I sent you two boats and a helicopter.'

Source: Anecdotal, author unknown.

Reflection

The moral of this tale could be 'Don't trust in the Lord' or 'Trust only in yourself' or possibly 'Watch out for signs that you are given.' I leave it to you to debate!

This story could be used for:

Empowerment/engagement.

Perceptions.

Positive thinking.

Realistic goal setting.

Self-belief.

Talking points

What is the message of the story?

What was the man's understanding of 'trusting in the Lord'?

Was his belief empowering or limiting?

Can you relate this sort of blind-faith belief to your own organization?

39 Watch the borders

This is a story that cautions against misunderstandings in communication – but also illustrates the power of urban legend and myth that permeate many organizations and communities.

J Edgar Hoover, the head of the FBI in the United States, had a reputation for being a demanding boss – particularly when it came to his insistence on neatly presented work. He ordered his assistants to type their memos leaving wide margins on either side of the paper so that he could write comments in the bright blue ink that was reserved solely for his use.

One day, so the story goes, an untrained assistant filled the page to the edges so that Hoover barely had room for any comment. He responded by returning the page to her, with just one line written at the bottom of the sheet: 'Watch the borders.'

According to the legend, hundreds of FBI agents were sent out to monitor the borders with Mexico and Canada to watch for anything suspicious. The reality is slightly less dramatic – while the memo and the ensuing confusion it caused were certainly true, the matter was relatively quickly cleared up after a few anxious phone calls to and from the various branches of the FBI.

Reference: Anecdotal. References on www.wikipedia.org and www.american_almanac.com.

Reflection

This story could be used for:

Communication.

Perceptions.

Leadership.

Teamwork.

Talking points

What does the story tell you about Hoover's leadership style?

Had he been more approachable and less demanding, might the story have ended differently?

What sort of problems can arise from misunderstandings of this sort?

Do you imagine that Hoover learnt anything from the occurrence?

What urban legends pervade your organization? Are they damaging?

40 The manager who succumbed to a staff attitude survey

I am indebted to Dr Peter Honey, with whom I share a love of stories and storytelling, for this tale.

Nigel was a director who managed (he would undoubtedly have said 'led') a factory assembling computers and IT hardware. Most of the staff were women doing fairly intricate work with circuit boards and the like, but, as is so often the way, all the managers and unit heads were men.

One day, Nigel went to a seminar where the speaker waxed lyrical about the benefits of staff attitude surveys and upward feedback. Nigel was attracted by the concept, not for himself but for his direct reports, many of whom he found wanting. So, he hired an outside consultant to conduct an attitude survey among all the staff.

A detailed questionnaire invited staff anonymously to say what they thought about everything from the food in the canteen to the quality of their managers. The staff, not used to being consulted or listened to, relished the opportunity to have their say. The questionnaires were analysed and the consultant went to see Nigel to give him a preliminary overview of the data. He said, 'I can summarize the findings by telling you that the majority of your staff are very critical of management in general and you in particular. Not to put too fine a point on it, they think you are an out and out bastard.'

Nigel was shocked to hear this. How could he be so seriously misunderstood? The consultant reassured Nigel that this was not at all unusual. He said he would help to put together a plan that would change the staff's perceptions for the better. The plan was simple: for one year, Nigel would spend one hour each working day talking with staff, asking for their ideas and being seen to listen. After the year, the attitude survey would be repeated so that the improvement could be measured.

So, for a year, Nigel applied his charm and diligently implemented the plan. He was genuinely surprised by the quality of the ideas that were forthcoming from his staff. Some of them resulted directly in cost-saving efficiencies.

The time came to repeat the attitude survey and analyse the results. Again the consultant met with Nigel to review the trends. He said, 'I am pleased to tell you that there has been some improvement. The majority of your staff now think you are a cunning bastard.'

Reference: An extract from Peter Honey's book, *50 Cautionary Tales for Managers* (2006), HowTo Books.

Reflection

As Peter says in his book, 'People aren't stupid.' We need to question the purpose and motives behind the carrying out of any survey, and also any resultant change in behaviour.

This story could be used for:

Communication.

Perceptions.

Leadership.

Teamwork.

Integrity/humility.

Talking points

Was it a good idea to have an attitude survey commissioned as the story relates? Would it not have been better to 'leave well alone'?

If you have had attitude surveys carried out recently, how have you used the information? (As many as 70 per cent of surveys are carried out but never acted upon.)

Was Nigel 'misunderstood', as he claimed?

What leadership style characterizes your organization?

HAPPY ENDINGS

This final collection of tales is intended to relax, surprise, entertain, make us feel that life is worth living or just make us laugh! There are no 'Reflection' and 'Talking points' sections after the tales. However, they can still be used productively during a workshop, as 'fill-ins', to bridge to your next topic, after lunch (the notorious graveyard spot) or at the end of a training session, to energize or to leave participants on a high. And of course, there's still nothing to say you can't use them for discussion purposes if you so wish. As the group title suggests, this collection of tales might have a twist or an unexpected, but hopefully happy, ending.

41 Marjorie's story

A friend of mine, Marjorie Burton, is a wonderful raconteur. This is one of those family stories that is told so often it gets its own name – 'the lilo story' – and I asked Marjorie to recount her memories of it.

I'd gone for a short holiday to the south of France with my daughter Ann and small granddaughter Louise. We were staying on a caravan site somewhere between St Tropez and Cannes; the weather was wonderful and we spent most of our days on the beach, which was gorgeous. One day, while we were on the beach, Ann said to me, 'You're looking a bit tired, Mum. Why don't you lie out on the lilo and have a rest for a bit?' This seemed like a good idea, so Ann blew up the inflatable lilo for me and I paddled out into the sea – just a little way because I didn't swim at all in those days and I was quite nervous of being in the water. I stretched out on the lilo. The sun was glorious, and after a short while I started to relax, closed my eyes and began to doze...

Imagine my horror when I woke up some time later and found that the shore had all but vanished. It looked to be miles away. I sat bolt upright, grabbing both sides of the lilo, feeling completely out of control, like a beached whale. I thought, 'This is going to be the end. I'm never going to see Ann or Louise again.' I kept staring in the direction of the shore. How on earth could I get back? If only I could swim... I looked around me in desperation – was there anyone who might help? Then, out of nowhere, I noticed a young Frenchman and his girlfriend, not that far away from me. They were splashing about in the water, playing ball, laughing and shouting to each other.

Mustering up my limited French, I waved frantically. '*Excusez-moi!*' I shouted to the man. And then, the extent of my French exhausted, lifted up the rope at the corner of the lilo and held it out to him pathetically. 'Can you help me back to the shore?'

'*Oui, bien sûr,*' replied the man. As he was nodding at the same time, I assumed that meant 'Yes.' He took hold of the rope and together he and his girlfriend began to pull the lilo – with me sitting on it regally, if a little unsteadily – back to the shore. But no sooner had the exercise started than my feelings of relief were overtaken by ones of confusion. I managed to tap the Frenchman on the arm as he continued to pull the lilo.

'Are you walking?' I asked him, in English. 'Yes, of course!' he said cheerily, as though stating the obvious, and as he spoke, I could see the water was only actually a few feet deep. As we approached the shore like a rather bizarre royal procession, I also noticed my daughter, not wailing and grieving for her mother lost at sea, as I might have imagined, but doubled up with laughter. She had seen everything. Trying to retain what little dignity I had left, I stepped off the lilo, thanked the rather bemused couple, and walked the remaining distance to the shore.

Soon after that holiday, I took swimming lessons. Luckily, no one asked me why I was so keen to learn.

Source: Marjorie Burton, story-gathering interview.

42 'Father and Child'

I remember first hearing this extract from the poem 'A Woman Young and Old' while studying English Literature at college. There was a mixed reaction after our tutor read it out. All the women in the group said, 'Aaaaaaahhh' in unison and all the men looked round vacantly, saying, 'What?' I suppose it must be a girl thing.

> She hears me strike the board and say
> That she is under ban
> Of all good men and women,
> Being mentioned with a man
> That has the worst of all bad names;
> And thereupon replies
> That his hair is beautiful,
> Cold as the March wind his eyes.

Reference: Extract from *The Works of W B Yeats* (1994), Wordsworth Editions.

43 Mother and the grapes

Some people ask where I get my somewhat eccentric view on life. Those of you who read my first book, Tales for Trainers, *will remember my late mother's rather unfortunate escapades with the knife grinder – and understand what I've inherited.*

'This is a good idea for New Year's Eve,' my mother announced one afternoon. Receiving a less than rapturous response from the family, she continued: 'It was in the *Reader's Digest*,' as though that gave the whole concept she was about to announce far more gravitas.

'Just before midnight,' she read, 'you get a bowl of 12 grapes, and as soon as the clocks chime midnight you start to eat them.'

'Why?' asked my sister, always the cynical one.

'Because for each one you eat while the clocks are still chiming, you will have a happy month in the new year!' replied Mother, her voice taking on the bubbling tone of an excited three-year-old, waiting her turn to see Santa. We already upheld one tradition religiously on New Year's Eve. Mother, being half Scottish and half Yorkshire, insisted on the custom of 'first footing' – that weird pastime that dictates that one person in the house (usually the person with the darkest hair) shall be the first one to cross the threshold in the new year, bearing a lump of coal, a sprig of holly, some fruitcake and a glass of whisky (all deeply symbolic). We could sense that this new addition to the festivities that Mother was now proposing was going to prove tricky to coordinate, but we agreed to humour her eccentricities and go along with it.

On the evening in question, my sister, being the darkest-haired of the family, was as usual ceremoniously ushered out of the front door at 11.55 pm and as Mother didn't believe in wasting heat, the door was firmly shut in her wake, leaving her standing shivering in the winter's cold, clutching the aforementioned articles, *plus* of course the additional burden of a small bowl containing 12 grapes. This unwilling exile was occasionally punctuated with a lifting of the letter box through which a pathetic voice could be faintly heard: 'Is it time yet?'

On the first stroke of midnight we heard the bells of Big Ben begin to chime on the television, and Mother shouted, '*Now!*' loud enough surely to scare the neighbours into suspecting a nuclear attack at the very least. She and I both proceeded to stuff the grapes into our mouths as fast as we could. (Strange how, looking back on the event, you realize you have become so engrossed in something that it just doesn't occur to you to stop and think of any sensible reason why you're doing it.)

Unfortunately, in her eagerness to try out this new and daring activity, Mother, as was her wont, had not really thought the thing through or, indeed, read the small print in the article, which, had she done so, would probably have advised, 'Seedless grapes would be preferable.' So now, alongside the continuing drone in the background of 'Is it time yet?' still emanating from behind the front door, a new sound was added to the cacophony – that of Mother and I chewing and swallowing grapes for all we were worth, spitting out the unexpected and unwelcome pips and gasping for air like a pair of synchronized swimmers.

Mother later deemed the whole event a huge success. She had triumphantly finished off her 12 grapes (although if we're honest, it was some time after Big Ben had stopped chiming). I think I managed to consume about three – I was laughing so much I was in serious danger of starting the New Year in casualty with someone performing the Heimlich manoeuvre on me. My sister, needless to say, was in a pretty black humour when finally allowed to re-enter the house, complete with the lump of coal, the now partially wilted sprig of holly, a half-eaten piece of fruitcake and an empty glass that once contained whisky ... oh, and 12 grapes – still intact.

Source: Family story.

44 The courageous grandma

This apparently true story featured on the internet recently; no doubt, in true storytelling fashion, it has been elaborated as time has gone on.

An elderly Florida lady was doing her shopping, and upon returning to her car found four young men in the act of leaving with her vehicle. She dropped her shopping bags and drew a handgun, proceeding to scream at the top of her voice, 'I have a gun, and I know how to use it! Get out of the car!'

The four men didn't wait for a second invitation. They got out and ran like mad. The lady, somewhat shaken, then proceeded to load her shopping bags into the back of the car and got into the driver's seat. She was so shaken that she could not get her key into the ignition. She tried and tried, and then it dawned on her why...

A few minutes later, she found her own car parked four or five spaces further down. She loaded her bags into the car and drove to the police station. The sergeant to whom she told the story couldn't stop laughing. He pointed to the other end of the counter, where four pale men were reporting a carjacking by a mad, elderly woman described as white, under five feet tall, glasses, curly white hair, and carrying a large handgun. No charges were filed.

Source: unknown.

45 An accidental discovery

This true story about one of the world's greatest scientists just goes to show that keeping your working area neat and tidy is not always productive.

Alexander Fleming, although known as a brilliant researcher, was not the tidiest of workers. His day-to-day materials – Petri dishes, tubes and other paraphernalia – were dumped in a big pile, which he would clean up every two or three weeks. He had been investigating the properties of staphylococci for some time and had taken a few weeks off to holiday with his family.

On returning from holiday, in September 1928, Fleming was just about to start his usual housekeeping routine when he noticed that one culture, in among the 30 or 40 plates scattered on his desk, was contaminated with a blue fungus. He later identified the mould as 'Penicillium notatum', and named the substance it discharged 'penicillin'.

Some years later, when he was visiting a modern research laboratory, Fleming observed with interest the sterile conditions that the scientists worked in.

'I bet you wish you'd had a place like this to work in,' said his guide proudly. 'Just think what you might have discovered.'

Fleming smiled wryly. 'Well, certainly not penicillin,' he replied.

Reference: Articles in www.wikipedia.co.uk.

46 I know we'll hear from you

All of us have at least one teacher that we remember clearly from our schooldays – that one individual who inspired us, believed in us, encouraged us in our learning. Sadly, Mrs Cross fitted into none of those categories. As I recall, she was a somewhat lumpen, mousy, unexceptional-looking woman in her late forties, who taught me and my hapless colleagues what was then called Domestic Science and Needlecraft, neither of which pursuits, it has to be said, were my particular forte. To her credit, she did struggle valiantly over the years to excite me in the joys of making real custard, Cornish pasties and soup, but sadly, most of it was lost on me and my culinary ineptitude. When it was time for the girls in my year to leave the school at the age of 18, Mrs Cross made a point of singling me out and shaking me by the hand.

'Goodbye, my dear,' she said, smiling, and then added sagely, 'I know we'll hear from you again.'

I was for a moment somewhat mystified at this prophetic comment, and then the light dawned on me. She had confused me, as many did, with my elder sister, known for her interest and enthusiasm in all things literary, and with whom there was a passing resemblance.

'No, I think you're mistaken, Mrs Cross,' I replied. 'You're confusing me with my sister. She's the one who writes.'

Mrs Cross continued to hold my hand, and looked me directly in the eye with a clarity and determination I had never noticed before.

'Oh no, my dear,' she said softly but firmly. 'I know who you are.'

Source: Family story.

47 Cinderella goes to the ball

Suddenly there was a flash of light, and in front of Cinderella stood a man dressed in loose-fitting, all cotton clothes and wearing a wide-brimmed hat.

'Hello, Cinderella,' said the man. 'I am your fairy godperson; I understand you want to go to the ball, eh? Do you really want to subject yourself to the male concept of beauty? Squeeze into some tight-fitting dress that will cut off your circulation? Jam your feet into high-heeled shoes that will ruin your bone structure? Paint your face with toxic chemicals?'

'Oh yes, please! Definitely!' said Cinderella without hesitation. The fairy godperson heaved a sigh and decided to postpone the political education until another day.

Reference: An extract from *Politically Correct Bedtime Stories* (1994) by James Finn Garner, published by Macmillan Publishing Company, New York.

48 Love letters

My father-in-law, Edwin Parkin, is known as a great raconteur and likes nothing better than to reminisce about his time in the RAF during the Second World War. I thought a while ago I'd heard all his stories, but this was one he must have been keeping up his sleeve. No doubt it's become embroidered in the telling (in true storytelling fashion) and sadly, my mother-in-law, Kathleen, is no longer with us to correct him (as she used to). But nevertheless, it's an enduring love story – and I think she would approve of his telling of it.

We'd been married for about 20 years, and sitting reminiscing one night about various people, going through some old photographs, I said to Kathleen, reflectively, 'Aaaaah … Nellie Schofield … I've a lot to thank her for.'

'Nellie Schofield?' said Kathleen.

'Yes, you must remember her. She was the one who sent me that letter.'

'Oh … yes … the letter,' said Kathleen.

Kathleen and I had originally got engaged in 1941 just before I was posted to Malta. All the time I was there, we were writing to each other regularly, every day. And then when I came home we went out together for some time. But sadly, things didn't work out and we broke it off.

Not long afterwards I went abroad again, to the Far East. You could say I had something of a roaming commission in those days – I went from Calcutta, through Burma to Rangoon, to Singapore and then to Java. All the time I'd been in Malta I'd been writing letters religiously, night after night. Now that I had no girlfriend, I thought, maybe a bit petulantly, at least there'd be none of that writing letters stuff. I hardly ever wrote home, except for the odd obligatory letter to my mother. And I didn't get any letters either, except an occasional one back from my mother every couple of months.

When I was in Java, the senior NCOs had their own mess. As I remember, it was a big house with a rather grand driveway. In the entrance to the building was the post room, and there was a wall of pigeonholes, all in alphabetical order, where they sorted out the mail. Well, of course, I didn't write to anyone and no one wrote to me, so I never bothered even looking in the post room. There was only one other chap in the mess at the time whose surname began with P. He used to say to me, 'Don't you ever get any mail, Eddie?' 'No,' I said, emphatically and rather brusquely. 'I don't get any and I don't write any,' in the tone of voice that told him I didn't want to continue the conversation.

One particular day, I went into the mess as usual at lunchtime. There were about 12 of us sitting round the table, and this chap (the other 'P') came in and said with great excitement, 'Guess what? There's a letter for Eddie!'

I snarled at him, brushing him away dismissively. 'Throw it away. It'll just be a bill that's caught up with me!'

'Ah no – not this one!' said the chap, smelling the envelope. 'It smells of perfume. This is from a girl!'

Without giving it to me, he passed it the next man at the lunch table, who also gave it a mock sniff. 'Yes ... definitely perfume,' he teased. It went all the way round the table before it was eventually passed to me.

I scuttled off to the semi-privacy of my bunk to read it. I couldn't believe the number of crossings-out on the envelope. It had been addressed to Sgt E Parkin, 591737 and had gone first of all to China; that address had been crossed out and the letter had been sent to Calcutta; that address was then crossed out and the letter sent to Rangoon, where the address was crossed out again and the letter sent to Singapore; that address too had been crossed out, and finally the letter had caught up with me in Java. It was a miracle that it ever got to me. The letter had been mailed in October 1945 and I received it in July 1946.

Nervously I opened it. Inside, an unknown hand had written:

Dear Edwin,

You don't know me but I'm a workmate of your former fiancée Kathleen. She's always talking about you and saying how sad she is now that the engagement is broken off. If you're not in a relationship and if you still think anything about her, please drop her a line. I'm sure she'd be over the moon.

Yours,

Nellie Schofield

Needless to say, I got my writing pad out and wrote back to Kathleen straight away, a three-page letter. The next day I wrote another, and then another...

Back in Barnsley, Kathleen's mother said to her when she returned home from work one day, 'He ought to have more sense. Look, there are three letters from him.'

'Letters from who?' said Kathleen.

'Edwin,' said her mother. 'I tell you – he should have more sense!'

Apparently, after we'd split up, Kathleen had started going out with another boy. But as soon as she got my letters, she met him the next night and said, 'I'm sorry – it's off.'

So eventually we got married in August 1947 and had many very happy years together – and all thanks to Nellie Schofield.

'Ah yes, I remember her now,' said Kathleen. 'Actually, I've got a confession to make about Nellie Schofield and that letter.'

'A confession?' I asked, coming out of my reverie. 'What sort of confession?'

'Well,' said Kathleen hesitantly. 'Nellie did *write* the letter – but actually I dictated it.'

There was a moment's silence. I thought I'd give it just long enough for her to worry that I was going to sue for divorce ... and then we both started laughing. I hugged Kathleen and said, 'I've still got a lot to thank her for.'

Source: Family story.

49 The story of a sign
(Historia de un letrero)

I have attempted to put into a narrative format the content of a short film, Historia de un letrero, *by Mexican film maker Alonso Álvarez Barreda, aged 24. The film won an award at the Cannes film festival in 2008.*

It is a beautiful, warm summer's day. Couples are walking through the park, children are running and playing, bursting balloons and chasing pigeons. On the ground sits an old man, a blind beggar. In front of him are a collecting tin and a handwritten cardboard sign that says, 'Show compassion. I am blind.' But the tin is empty; people in the park are walking past him, perhaps embarrassed, perhaps too busy to stop. One young man throws a cigarette butt into the tin with contempt.

But then a young businessman walks into the park. He straightens his tie and checks his watch, obviously heading for an important meeting. He passes the blind man, but then stops and comes back and stands and looks at him. The blind man knows there is someone there. He reaches out and feels the shoes – they are smart and polished, unlike his own tattered trainers. The young man takes out a pen and, reaching for the cardboard sign, he turns it over and writes a new message on the other side. He pats the old man on the shoulder and walks away.

Now everyone seems to be coming up to the blind man and putting money into his tin. He can hear the coins and notes as they clank and rustle. Soon the tin is overflowing, and he is incredulous, overjoyed and laughing as he scoops the money off the ground.

The young businessman returns, and this time he bends down to talk to the old blind man.

'What did you do to my sign?' the old man asks.

'I wrote the same as you – but in different words,' the young man replies. He holds up the cardboard sign which now reads: 'Today is a beautiful day and I cannot see it.'

Reference: *Historia de un letrero*, film by Alonso Álvarez Barreda: www.historiadeunletrero.com.

50 One for the road

A final story from Birbal, Indian poet and author, demonstrating the continuing power of stories and storytelling.

The emperor Akbar was travelling to a distant place along with some of his courtiers. It was a hot day and the emperor was tiring of the journey.

'Can't anybody make this journey shorter?' he asked, with an irritated tone.

'I can,' said Birbal.

The other courtiers looked at one another, perplexed. All of them knew there was no other path through the hilly terrain. The road they were travelling on was the only one that could take them to their destination.

'You can shorten the road?' said the emperor. 'Well, do it.'

'I will,' said Birbal. 'Listen first to this story I have to tell.' And riding beside the emperor, he launched upon a long and intriguing tale that held Akbar and all those listening spellbound. Before they knew it they had reached the end of their journey.

'We're here?' exclaimed Akbar. 'So soon!'

'Indeed, master,' smiled Birbal. 'You did say you wanted the road to be shortened.'

Reference: A retold traditional Indian folk tale. More Indian folk tales can be found at www.dimdima.com.

References and further reading

Atkinson, P E (1990) Creating cultural change, *Management Services*, **34**, pp 6–10

Bettelheim, B (1991) *The Uses of Enchantment: the Meaning and Importance of Fairy Tales*, Knopf, New York, USA

Booker, C (2004) *The Seven Basic Plots: Why We Tell Stories*, Continuum Publishing

Borton, T (1970) *Reach, Touch and Teach*, McGraw-Hill Education

Bruner, J (1990) Culture and human development: a new look, *Human Development*, **33**, pp 344–55

Campbell, J (1993) *The Hero with a Thousand Faces*, Fontana Press, London

Campbell, J and Moyers, B (1988) *The Power of Myth*, Doubleday, New York

Cialdini, R (2007) *Yes! 50 Secrets from the Science of Persuasion*, Profile Books

Csikszentkihalyi, M (1990) *Flow: The Psychology of Optimal Experience*, Harper & Row, New York

Denning, S (2001) *The Springboard – How Storytelling Ignites Action in Knowledge-era Organizations*, Butterworth Heinemann

Denning, S (2005) *The Leader's Guide to Storytelling*, Jossey-Bass, San Francisco, CA

Denning, S (2007) *The Secret Language of Leadership*, Jossey-Bass, San Francisco, CA

Garfield, S (2006) 10 reasons why people don't share their knowledge, *Knowledge Management Review*, May/June

Geldof, B (1986) *Is That It?*, Sidgwick & Jackson, London

Gibbs, G (1988) *Learning by Doing: A guide to teaching and learning methods*, Further Education Unit, Oxford Polytechnic, Oxford

Gordon, D (1978) *Therapeutic Metaphors*, Meta Publications, USA

Grant, D and Oswick, C (1996) *Metaphor and Organization*, Sage Publications

Greenberg, C L, Williams, Col. T J and Baker, D (2007) Thinking with the whole brain: http://www.ksg.harvard.edu/leadership/Pdf/ThinkingWithThe WholeBrain.pdf

Hibbard, C (2009) *Stories that Sell*, Aim Publishers, USA

Honey, P (2006) *50 Cautionary Tales for Managers*, HowTo Books

Hsu, J (2008) The secrets of storytelling, *Scientific American Journal*, August/September

Jensen, E (1995) *The Learning Brain*, Turning Point Publishing, USA

Johnson, G (1992) Managing strategic change – culture and actions, *Long Range Planning*, 25, p 31

Ketner, M G (2001) *Lifetimes: the Texas experience*, UTSA's Institute of Texan Cultures

Kleiner, A and Roth, G (1997) How to make experience your company's best teacher, *Harvard Business Review* on knowledge management, HBS Press

Kolb, D A (1985) *Experiential Learning: Experience as the Source of Learning and Development*, Prentice Hall

Kovecses, Z (2002) *Metaphor: A Practical Introduction*, Oxford University Press, Oxford

Labonte and Featherstone (1997) The story dialogue method: article featured in www.evaluationtrust.org/tools/story

Lakoff, G and Johnson, M (1980) *Metaphors We Live By*, University of Chicago Press

Maguire, J (1998) *The Power of Personal Storytelling*, Tarcher/Putnam, USA

Matthew, R and Wacker, W (2008) *What's Your Story?*, Pearson Education

Morgan, G (1997) *Images of Organization*, Sage Publications

Nadler, L and Nadler, Z (1990) *The Handbook of Human Resource Development*, Wiley, New York

Neuhauser P, (1993) *Corporate Legends and Lore*, McGraw-Hill, New York, USA

Parkin, M (1998) *Tales for Trainers – Using Stories and Metaphors to Facilitate Learning*, Kogan Page, London

Parkin, M (2001) *Tales for Coaching – Using Stories and Metaphors with Individuals and Small Groups*, Kogan Page, London

Parkin, M (2004) *Tales for Change – Using Storytelling to Develop People and Organizations*, Kogan Page, London

Petrova, P K and Cialdini R B (2005) Fluency of consumption imagery and the backfire effects of imagery appeals, *Journal of Consumer Research*, **32**, pp 442–52

Pink, D (2008) *A Whole New Mind*, Marshall Cavendish, USA

Reps, P (2000) *Zen Flesh, Zen Bones*, Penguin Publishing, London

Rosen, B (1988) *And None of It Was Nonsense*, Mary Glasgow, London

Rossing, B E and Long, H B (1981) Contributions of curiosity and relevance to adult learning motivation, *Adult Education*, **32** (1), Fall, pp 25–36

Senge, P (1990) *The Fifth Discipline: The Art and Practice of The Learning Organization*, Doubleday/Currency

Shah, I (1983) *The Exploits of the Incomparable Mulla Nasrudin*, Octagon Press

Schein, E H (1985) *Organizational Culture and Leadership: A Dynamic View*, Jossey-Bass, San Francisco, CA

Silverman, L (2006) *Wake Me Up When the Data Is Over*, Jossey-Bass, San Francisco, CA

Simmons, A (2006) *The Story Factor*, Basic Books, New York

Snowden, D J (2000) The art and science of story, or 'Are you sitting comfortably?', Part 2: The weft and warp of purposeful story, first published in *Business Information Review*, **17** (4), December

Thurber, J (1943) *Many Moons*, Harcourt Children's Books

Turnball, C (1961) *Forest People*, Jonathan Cape, London

Further information

Margaret Parkin can be contacted at info@success-stories.co.uk or through the website at www.success-stories.co.uk, where you'll also find more stories, tips and techniques and a free newsletter. Alternatively you can listen to Margaret telling stories on the Kogan Page website: www.koganpage.com.

This is what we offer at Success Stories:

Business coaching

We work with senior and middle managers to help them clarify and achieve their goals, build self-esteem, manage staff more effectively, give memorable presentations, resolve conflict or improve team effectiveness.

Training and development

We run half- and full-day workshops in leadership, and in management and personal development, using stories and metaphors as a key part of the learning methodology. We also run public master-class workshops in business storytelling.

Consultancy

We use narrative research techniques with staff and customers to determine the health of an organization; we also identify, gather and craft 'Success stories' from your customers and staff to be used for internal and external marketing purposes.

Keynote speeches

Margaret is an accredited speaker with Women Speakers' Agency, the UK and Europe's premier speaker bureau promoting the most outstanding women speakers and conference hosts/facilitators. Visit: www.womenspeakers.co.uk.

Index

NB: page numbers in *italic* indicate figures or tables